AMERICAN HERITAGE
ILLUSTRATED HISTORY
OF THE UNITED STATES

William D. Peck, a gold miner who lived in Rough and Ready, California, sat for this painting in 1852 in his own well-stocked but simple cabin.

FRONT COVER: B-Troop Leaving San Carlos *is the title of this oil painting by Francis H. Beaugureau.*
FROM THE COLLECTION OF HARRISON EITELJORG

FRONT ENDSHEET: *On August 23, 1862, the Sioux under Chief Little Crow attacked the town of New Ulm, killing farmers harvesting grain in the fields.*
MINNESOTA STATE CAPITOL

CONTENTS PAGE: *A cowboy rides the day herd as the northbound cattle graze.*
HISTORICAL SOCIETY OF MINNESOTA

BACK ENDSHEET: *Mexican Vaqueros are trying to round up a thundering herd of wild horses. Once they were caught, the horses were broken and trained.*
COLLECTION OF CARL S. DENTZEL

BACK COVER: (*top left*) *Sioux Chief Sitting Bull; famed U.S. Cavalryman and Civil War hero George A. Custer* (*top right*), *who died in ''Custer's Last Stand'' when overwhelmed by Sitting Bull's warriors; the Charles M. Russell painting of the solitary cowboy* (*bottom*) On Day Herd No. 2.
THE THOMAS GILCREASE INSTITUTE OF AMERICAN HISTORY AND ART, TULSA, OKLAHOMA; LIBRARY OF CONGRESS

AMERICAN HERITAGE ILLUSTRATED HISTORY OF THE UNITED STATES

VOLUME 9

WINNING THE WEST

BY ROBERT G. ATHEARN

Created in Association with the
Editors of AMERICAN HERITAGE

and for the updated edition
MEDIA PROJECTS INCORPORATED

CHOICE PUBLISHING INC.

New York·

Library of Congress Catalog Card Number: 87-73399
ISBN 0-945260-09-1

This 1988 edition is published and distributed by Choice Publishing, Inc., 53 Watermill Lane, Great Neck, NY 11021
by arrangement with American Heritage, a division of Forbes, Inc.

Manufactured in the United States of America

CONTENTS OF THE COMPLETE SERIES

Editor's Note to the Revised Edition
Introduction by ALLAN NEVINS
Main text by ROBERT G. ATHEARN

EACH VOLUME CONTAINS AN ENCYCLOPEDIC SECTION; MASTER INDEX IN VOLUME 18

CONTENTS OF VOLUME 9

CHAPTER 25

Search for El Dorado

The Civil War temporarily diverted public attention from the trans-Mississippi West and from its great promise as an area of expansion and a source of wealth for the United States. The prewar years had offered only a brief and tantalizing period of assessment, just long enough to arouse curiosity about the region's boundless opportunities but far too short to do much about exploiting them. Gold had created the state of California in 1850; nine years later, the pioneer farmers of the Willamette Valley banded together to put Oregon into the Union. But between these two outposts on the Pacific and the other states was a vast area, largely unpopulated and largely unknown. Almost none of the West's long-range agricultural possibilities had been examined, and only a part of its mineral deposits had been discovered.

During the brief span of time between the Mexican War and the Civil War, the only important attempts to farm any of the country beyond the Missouri were made in Oregon, in certain areas of Colorado, Nevada, and California to meet the demands of mining communities, and, incredibly, in the barren and forbidding valley of the Great Salt Lake. The Mormons, driven from their homes in the East by religious persecution, had reached this area in 1847—even before the United States had acquired its new empire in the Southwest. In a short time these industrious and resourceful people had literally "made the desert bloom" in the first large-scale demonstration of what irrigation could do.

The most important pre-Civil War activity in the West, however, was mining. Hardly had the ink dried on the Treaty of Guadalupe Hidalgo before the forty-niners were streaming westward to dig for gold. Hard on their heels came the fifty-niners, who searched the mountains of Nevada and Colorado. Almost immediately after that, the mineral frontier spread to Idaho and Montana. But before the mining boom could reach its height, the war came. In a little over a decade, Americans had not been able to do

The lone gold prospector, his tools, pan, and provisions loaded on the back of his mule, was a familiar figure in California gold fields before the big mining companies began their large-scale operations.

KNOEDLER GALLERIES

much more than scratch the surface.

The Civil War did not halt prospecting. Instead, it stimulated mining because of the great demand for gold and silver by both the Union and Confederate governments—and because many a lad preferred digging for gold to carrying a rifle. But more permanent settling of the West had to wait until the war's end. Because few troops could be spared from the battlefields to protect the raw frontier from menacing Indians, the West was still a dangerous place to live in. Soaring prices for agricultural products made farming in the older, more settled areas of the East more profitable than ever before, and thus there was little incentive to seek new lands to the west. But in the long run, the war proved to be a great stimulus to Western migration.

Conquest of the West

Every family, North or South, had in some way been affected by the war. Although many Americans did not realize it at the time, the war was a revolution: A certain way of life was passing forever, and the country would never again be quite the same. Thousands of young men left home for the first time. After months, or even years, of life in the field, they were unwilling to return to the routine of farm or city life. In search of further adventures, they saw new opportunity in the sparsely populated areas of the West. Across the Missouri River they poured in search of jobs—as laborers on railroad-construction gangs, as cowboys on the new cattle ranches, as miners in the rich Montana gold fields, or as land speculators in the latest bonanza. Back East, Americans watched the progress and noted with satisfaction the appearance of one new state after the other across maps that had once read Great American Desert.

The conquest of America's Far West was to be no simple task. It was easy enough for Horace Greeley, sitting in his office at the *New York Tribune,* to say "Go west, young man," but a great many who took the famous editor at his word were sorely disappointed by what they found. It was not a place of glamour, excitement, and romance for the vast majority, who instead found hard work, dust, drought, bitter winters, sickness, and danger.

First of all, there were the still-hostile Indians. The tribesmen had no census takers, of course, but it is estimated that there were over 200,000 natives on the high plains and in the Rocky Mountain region alone. Strongest and most warlike of the northern tribes were the Sioux, Blackfeet, Cheyennes, Arapahoes, and Crows. South of the Platte River the Comanches, Kiowas, Utes, Southern Arapahoes, Navajos, and Apaches dominated the country all the way to Mexico. Thanks to the Spanish, the warriors of these tribes had horses, and on their swift, well-trained mounts they were formidable enemies. Before the Civil War, the Western Indians had had little contact with white men in any great numbers, and there had been few chances for friction to develop between the two races. The Indians of the plains and mountains had not objected strongly to the occasional wagon-train caravans that passed through their country on the way to Oregon or California. Understandably, they looked differently at the whites who came to stay in the years following the war. As these ever-increasing hordes of settlers started to fence in the land, slaughter the buffalo, and drive them into reservations, the Indians suddenly realized with fear and anger that their entire way of life was threatened. Rather than submit to this invasion, they were determined to resist—almost to the last man—and fierce wars between Indians and whites were to rage across the West until the closing decade of the 19th century.

Indians were not the only barrier to the Western movement. The population in this immense region was thin and scattered, and the government had little more than an uneasy grip on the land. Into this political vacuum came thousands of young men, free for the first time from the conventional restrictions and responsibilities of civilized life. Most of them were honest, law-abiding individuals, but many

In a painting by Frederic Remington, mounted Indians risk being shot down by cavalrymen as they race across the open plains to swoop up a fallen brave.

were not. Without the protection of traditional law-enforcement agencies, they were obliged to settle differences among themselves in their own way. Lacking policemen, courts, judges, and prisons, Westerners found that the best way to deal with lawless elements was to take the most direct action in the quickest time possible, and think about the consequences afterward. When this resulted in what appeared to be a too-liberal use of "hemp justice," older parts of America began calling the West "wild." The tendency to resort to personal settlement of a dispute with pistols (or six-shooters, to fans of modern Western adventure stories) did not help the new country's reputation.

The pioneering spirit

The men and women who survived Indian hostility and weathered the lawlessness of the frontier found that the rolling plains were best suited to ranching and not to the type of farming that they were used to in the rocky soil of the Northeast or in the rich earth of the Old South. It was not as if settlers could just move west and

In the early days, before courts were located in the West, citizens like these coming from a hanging, or "necktie party," took the law into their own hands.

Indians watch with suspicion on the banks of the Missouri River near Fort Berthold as a steamboat—or "fire canoe," as they called it—moves past them

take up their former way of life in a new setting. There was a vast difference, and even veteran farmers had much to learn.

These obstacles did more to sift out the weak and timid than they did to slow up the westward movement. Those who were determined to go west to make their fortunes were not going to let anything stand in their way, least of all poor and inadequate means of transportation. Those who were in a hurry, perhaps headed for the gold regions, went by wagon, by horseback, or even by foot. If one wanted to get to Montana, the best means was by water. Drab little

steamers drawing an amazingly small amount of water crabbed their way upriver, over sand bars and around snags clear to the head of navigation at Fort Benton. Although this means of travel was better than the prairie schooner, it had its limitations. When overtaxed, the steamers had an exasperating habit of blowing up, spewing their contents considerable distances.

Most of the Western immigrants went by rail. Service to the Pacific Coast was established as early as 1869, and within a few years, iron roads crisscrossed the entire West. Earlier homesteaders had gone forth as the spirit moved them, but the later legions often were persuaded by the railroads through an extensive and elaborate system of advertising. The comparative comfort and safety of the railroads induced thousands who might not have been willing to go by wagon to take the big step. More important, the railroads promised a means of shipping crops to market, and once assured of this, Eastern farmers overcame their reluctance to move west.

In the trans-Mississippi West, the usual order of pioneering was reversed. From the Atlantic to the Mississippi it had been the farmer who—after the fur trapper, of course—had moved out on the frontier first. On this final frontier, he was the last to come.

What upset the order was gold. Its discovery in California in 1848 and the expectation of making similar strikes in other Western areas lured men from their homes in the East as nothing else ever had. After California, it was Nevada, then Oregon and Idaho, and next Montana that beckoned the gold seekers. Thus the traditional "Westward ho!" became "Eastward ho!" as the California miners went to dig in Colorado or in the Black Hills of Dakota.

Stampede to the gold fields

There was no regular progression of the mining frontier, and it had no direction except by accident. The merest whisper of a rumor set off a wild stampede to any new El Dorado.

Men rushed to the site as if driven by demons, taking with them only the barest essentials. Why bother with food and extra clothes when tomorrow everyone would be a millionaire?

The California gold rush was not America's first experience in mining the precious metal, but it was the biggest and most spectacular bonanza the world had yet seen, and many a prospector learned his trade there. From California, pick-and-pan brigades fanned out to all parts of the West, as aggressive, as inquisitive, as persistent as ant trains at a picnic. One of the first new strikes in the outbound trek came close to the starting place, in Nevada.

A number of forty-niners crossing Nevada on their way to California had cast speculative eyes on the great Washoe Range, and particularly on its highest peak, Mount Davidson. A couple of ravines that ran down the mountainside had yielded bits of "color" in that great gold-rush year, but there was not enough promise in it to detain the miners on their way west. The youngsters of the Mormon battalion, heading back to Salt Lake City from California in 1848, may have found a few grains of gold in the region, but again not in any quantity. It was a decade after the forty-niners passed through Nevada before much gold was found on the eastern slopes of the Sierras. In the spring of 1859, several prospectors, including one named Henry Comstock, made their strike in one of Mount Davidson's ravines. The bluish rock in which they found gold proved to be worth $3,000 a ton—in silver. In the next 20 years, the fabulous Comstock Lode yielded $300,000,000, the richest single strike in mining history.

From across the Sierras, in Nevada County, California, came the first wave of prospectors. When the nation learned that an ore rich in both gold and silver was being mined in large amounts, Nevada found its place on the map.

A hard-drinking miner known as Old Virginny gave his name to Virginia City, the principal camp. Into this hastily built board-and-canvas "city" poured the miners. Many had never dug for silver and were totally unequipped to probe granite mountains for ore-bearing quartz. But even if they could not sink shafts without the machinery that would only come later, they staked off claims with wild abandon and sold "mines" right and left to newcomers. A good many who missed the first onrush, and came upon a camp well staked off, simply moved on looking for other diggings in the region. Some were successful. A group of men who had made a search south and east of Virginia City found gold deposits near the California state line and named their find Aurora. A couple of years later, another rush took place in central Nevada, along

America's first transcontinental train travels west in 1869 on Union Pacific rails. This Currier and Ives print shows it stopped at a small prairie town.

the Reese River, after a former pony-express rider named William Talcott reported promising color in that region. Like water seeping into crevices, these relentless men penetrated the most remote parts of the West in their search for the elusive yellow dust.

The high cost of gold mining

As the magical word Comstock floated eastward, the siren song of gold nuggets clinking in wash pans brought men to yet another mountain mining frontier. In 1858, the Russell brothers—Green, Oliver, and Levi—found encouraging color near modern Denver. The panning produced only a few hundred dollars, but it was better than anything they had found until then. Word of a big strike in the central Rockies—a story that was at the time without foundation—made its way back east. Restless Americans, concerned over the mounting sectional issue and plagued by the financial panic of 1857, found temporary escape in such reports, and thousands not content with mere talk about the reported discoveries headed west in the spring of 1859.

How many made the trek is anyone's guess, but one estimate is that 100,000 set out, about half reached the actual scene of mining operations, and about 25,000 of these returned home in disillusion. There was considerable muttering about the "Pikes Peak hoax," and the army of "go backs," who, meeting fresh recruits on their way to the mines, did all they

could to discourage them. Few who had made up their minds to go west were discouraged by such gloomy warnings. Fortunately for them, a substantial find was made by John H. Gregory in May, 1859, and the world had proof that Pikes Peak was no hoax. News of the Gregory strike along Clear Creek, north and west of Denver, swelled the numbers of Argonauts to invasion proportions.

Denver, never a mining camp itself, was almost depopulated. Businessmen left their shops and professional men locked their offices, a fact recorded in the first issue of the *Rocky Mountain News:* "A. F. Peck, M.D., Physician and Surgeon, Cache-a-La-Poudre, Nebraska [of which Colorado was yet a part], where he may at all times be found when not professionally engaged or digging gold." The young city of Denver soon recovered and even thrived as incoming merchants filled the ranks of the missing and made it a major supply point for the entire Pikes Peak region. Endlessly the wagon trains rolled in from the Missouri River, bringing the necessities of life to an army of miners. Eggs came packed in barrels of lard and sold for $2 a dozen; apples cost from 25¢ to 50¢ apiece. Buyers complained of the freight rates that varied from 6¢ to 25¢ a pound, a criticism that was repeated by merchants who blamed their high prices on transportation costs. A story is told of a Denver woman who was shocked at the price of candles. "Well, madam," the store-

Henry Comstock (seated at the left) stakes out the first claim on June 12, 1859, to the Comstock Lode in Nevada, worth $300,000,000 in the next 20 years.

keeper explained apologetically, "the Indian troubles on the plains are bad and freight rates are up." "What!" his customer exclaimed. "Are the Indians fighting by candlelight?"

In its earliest days, the mining region was wild and unregulated. "There are duels, shooting affrays, and hanging by mob law most every week, which keeps up a morbid excitement through the mines and towns," wrote a youngster from Pennsylvania who had come west for adventure. He admitted, however, that "no one who follows a legitimate business, tends only to his own affairs, or has any moral proclivities is in danger of these self-constituted vigilance committees or mob juries." The Colorado gold rush was like all the others, before and after it, in its shifting, temporary,

and erratic course as miners scurried from one diggings to the next. But this phase was as brief as it was violent. Within half a dozen years, the top had been taken off, and the serious quartz, or hard-rock, mining began. Those who lived by the pick and pan moved on to some new field, leaving behind little or no trace of their labors except a few rotting, crumbling shacks that would eventually turn to dust.

A good many of the Nevada and Colorado placer miners headed north —to Idaho, and then into Montana. In 1860, E. D. Pierce and a party of prospectors discovered gold along the Clearwater, a branch of the Snake River. The men returned to Walla Walla, an outfitting point, and bought enough supplies to grubstake their venture for the winter. When they

Equipped with all kinds of gadgets, some of them useless, a prospector comes west.

headed for the hills once more, they were followed by others who had heard the news. Within months, the Clearwater mines were sending $100,-000 worth of dust a month into Portland. By 1861, such places as Pierce City, Lewiston, and Oro Fino were being challenged by stripling newcomers. Men were excitedly discussing Elk City or Florence—now these were the camps with promise—and before long they were challenging their elders. Portland, eager to outdo its arch rival, San Francisco, boasted through its newspapers that the new

mines were richer than those discovered earlier in California, and men died in the snowdrifts, fighting their way to the reported mother lode. The summer of 1862 witnessed a rash of new mining camps in the Boise region, with the ever-present name of Placerville appearing on the map, along with Owyhee, Ruby City, and Silver City.

Eastward, across the Beaverhead Range, lay a vast land soon to bear the name Montana. It was the next target for the miners, and by 1862 it was time for a new stampede. The placer mines of California, Oregon, Nevada, and Colorado had been thoroughly worked over, and there were even nervous rumblings of diminishing returns in the relatively new Idaho camps. There had been evidences of gold in Montana as early as 1852, but they were scant and the distances to the reported sites were great. By the 1860s, however, Lieutenant John Mullan had surveyed his road from Fort Benton to the headwaters of the Columbia River, by way of Hell Gate (modern Missoula), opening the way for the establishment of transportation facilities. Even better, Fort Benton was now the head of navigation on the Missouri River, and this little prairie port of call was only about 100 miles from future mining country.

A $5,000,000 strike

Montana gold mining got off to a fast start when John White discovered gold along Grasshopper Creek, a tributary of the Missouri, in July, 1862.

734

A cartoon jibes at the high cost of food in the gold fields of California. The merchants who supplied provisions often became richer than the miners.

Almost overnight the town of Bannack appeared, and by the following spring, around 1,000 men were at work, panning the gravel of the creek bed. Some $5,000,000 in dust is said to have been extracted from the strike during the first year of operation. Then came the by now familiar sequel: A new find was made nearby—one reported to be even richer—and men fled the town as if a plague had settled upon it.

The discovery that gave birth to Virginia City, Montana—one of the hell-roaringest camps in the West—

was made by accident. In the spring of 1863, a group of miners at Bannack determined to explore the region of the Yellowstone River in the hope of finding new and better diggings. But they were chased out by the Crow Indians, and as a fragment of the expedition made its way back toward Bannack, the men stopped here and there to try their luck at panning. One day in May, they crossed the divide between the Madison and Stinking Water Rivers, and finding a heavy stand of grass along a little creek, they decided to rest up and care for

The scene is the Hurdy-Gurdy House in Virginia City, Montana. Here the miners provided themselves with the amusements they missed while out prospecting.

some of the horses that had gone lame. To kill time, some of the party moved up the creek to pan, leaving behind Bill Fairweather and Henry Edgar, whose turn it was to stand duty —that is, take care of the horses and guard the supplies. Fairweather noticed a piece of rimrock sticking up on a creek-bed bar and took a few swings at it with his pick, after which he dumped some of the loose soil into a pan. "Now go and wash that pan and see if you can get enough to buy some tobacco when we get to town," he told Edgar. After a few deft motions, Edgar looked at the gleaming particles in the roiled water and knew he had found more than tobacco money. When he compared his results with those of Fairweather, who was also panning some of the soil, he dis-

covered that each had found $2.40 in one try. "Pretty good for tobacco money," Edgar wrote in his diary. When the others returned to camp, empty-handed, the pair who had stayed behind had exhilarating news.

Instant cities

Suppressing their excitement, the party hastened to Bannack for food and supplies, each sworn to deepest secrecy. But the gold dust they handed across the counter in return for the grubstake spoke for itself, and when the men slipped out of town, headed for the little campsite along Alder Gulch, most of Bannack followed at a respectful distance. To prevent absolute pandemonium, the miners pulled up and announced that they would go no further until some ground rules

736

were laid down for the rush they knew was coming. Accordingly, an agreement was made to protect the original discoverers, and a code of laws to govern the yet-to-be-born mining camp was drawn up. After the formalities came the rush, and another instant city appeared on the map. Overnight the gulch was staked off, rude tent-houses were built, and within a matter of days a long row of stores, hotels, saloons, dance halls, and two churches had appeared. It is small wonder that European visitors, accustomed to the slow, steady development of their cities, watched with amazement the crashing, helter-skelter progress of civic growth in the American West.

The rivers of humanity that poured into Virginia City, Montana, divided into little streams of men convinced that the direction they took would lead them to bigger and better bonanzas nearby. John Cowan and three other Southerners scoured the countryside, probing each likely ledge and every promising creek bed. Among those they investigated in west-central Montana was Prickly Pear Creek, a runlet that showed little promise at first glance. Leaving it, they moved on, exploring the Little Blackfoot River and even the Marias River, only to return with no further ideas except to give Prickly Pear one more try. In July, 1864, they found what they were looking for, and Last Chance Gulch became the new catchword among Montana miners. That autumn a general meeting was held, and the miners

In the best tradition of the West, what began as a friendly game of cards is about to end, after someone has cheated, in a fast and deadly gun battle.

renamed their city Helena. As before, the discovery spawned other camps around it, and soon Montana City, Jefferson City, Diamond City, and Confederate Gulch dotted the map.

The mineral frontier doubles back

The mineral frontier, as direction-less as a drop of mercury splashed on a table top, continued to find its way into the nooks and crannies of the West. Some of the Montana miners probed the Yellowstone Valley and, finding nothing, moved down along the mountains to the south, finally making an examination of the whole Wyoming segment of the Rockies. But no strike of any great size was ever made in Wyoming.

Late in the game, gold was discovered in quantity in South Dakota, the easternmost region of the mining frontier. During the winter of 1866–67, a number of soldiers organized the Black Hills Exploring and Mining Association to extract the yellow flakes they were sure they would find in the region. The federal government, harassed by Indian troubles, was re-solved to keep this new horde of pros-

Logs in the middle of the street, too many buckboards, and mud everywhere turned the main street of Deadwood, South Dakota, into confusion in 1876.

This procession was formed in Weaverville, California, in 1860, as part of a German May Day festival, giving the small mining town an international flavor.

pectors off reserved lands, and for a time the invasion was stalled. However, in the early '70s the fever was rising again, after Lieutenant Colonel George Custer's exploration in 1874 and his report that there were definite evidences of gold in that part of the country. Not even the United States Army could stop the ensuing rush, and by 1875 the soldiers found their task of escorting miners out of the country so futile that the whole idea was abandoned. From the winter of 1874–75 until about 1877, prospectors poured in, whipping together new mining towns, creating a new mineral frontier. Names like Custer City and Deadwood appeared on the map, and from them fresh legends grew—legends that have become a part of American folklore today. It was in Deadwood that Wild Bill Hickok died while playing poker, shot from behind, and it was there that Calamity Jane mourned his passing. Most of the stories about this mining camp are pure legend, but many poker players still call aces and eights, the cards Wild Bill was said to be holding in his last moments, the "dead man's hand."

To "git and git out"

Mining is an extractive industry—one in which everything is taken from the earth and nothing is put back. When the minerals that men seek can no longer be found, the site is abandoned in favor of a more promising one. All across the West today are hundreds of ghost towns, their bleached and sagging buildings evincing the changing fortunes of their former occupants.

There are comparatively few modern cities in the West whose origins can be traced back to mining camps. The few that survived after the gold and silver had run out did so because some new industry was developed to hold the population or because some new ore—less romantic, perhaps, but eventually to prove more profitable—was discovered in the vicinity. Butte, Montana, is the leading example of a former mining camp that still lives by mining. When their gold supply gave out, Butte residents turned to the far greater deposits of copper and found a supply large enough to last for generations.

But there are not many Buttes in the West. Bannack is almost forgotten today, and its rival, Virginia City, survives only because it is a tourist attraction. Helena, the former Last Chance Gulch, also exists for reasons other than mining; it is the state capital. The story is the same in Colorado, where the largest city, Denver, was never important as a mining camp. Such fabled places as Central City, Leadville, Cripple Creek, and Aspen, whose names were synonymous with bonanza, have long since lost that reputation. Now Central City and Aspen are resorts that preserve for vacationing Easterners a quaint sample of the Old West. This is virtually all that remains—outside of movie and television screens—to remind us of a fascinating chapter in American history. As the miners themselves admitted, they came to "git and git out."

The mining frontier was wasteful in many respects, but there is no doubt that it made a contribution to the development of American life. Aside from the gold and silver it pumped into the nation's financial bloodstream and the wealth or employment it created for a segment of our population, the industry stimulated other economic developments. Gold was the cornerstone; it first brought people to Nevada, Montana, Idaho, and Colorado. But just as the soldier in the field must be supported by those behind the lines, miners required a number of services. Merchants, professional men and women, teamsters, blacksmiths, stockmen, and farmers formed a kind of auxiliary corps in each of the successive mineral rushes. Supply centers grew into thriving cities, and farms appeared near the gold fields.

HISTORICAL SOCIETY OF MONTANA

COWBOYS—
LIFE ON THE RANGE

The cowboy is now a legend, and it is difficult to separate what he actually was from what he has come to mean today in the literature of the West. It is true that he lived bravely on the Great Plains, fighting the harsh and fickle weather, the constant threat of stampede, the plunder of Indians and outlaws. He worked hard, and when he came to town with his herd, he played hard and spent his money freely. Around these elements of truth, the legend of the cowboy has grown. What is not remembered about him is that his life was most often lonely, filled with the boredom of many days and nights when nothing happened, when he had little more than the simple resources of his own character to sustain him. It is as if the loneliness and boredom are forgotten because the cowboy's life at its most colorful expresses something basic to the American character— the compulsion to engage in endless movement in search of freedom and independence.

741

COWBOYS—LIFE ON THE RANGE

THE VAQUERO

The first American cowboy was called a vaquero. He was a mounted herdsman of Mexico and California, an Indian who had been trained by his Spanish masters to tend the increasing numbers of cattle on the mission ranchos. The vaquero above, typically outfitted in ankle-length pants that button up the sides, is busting, or throwing, a young bull. His horse is keeping the rope taut so that the frightened animal cannot stand up.

COWBOYS—LIFE ON THE RANGE

THE ROUNDUP

There were two roundups in the year. The first, in the spring, was to locate the cattle that had drifted during the winter and to brand new calves. The other took place in the fall to gather animals that were to go to market and again to find the lost cattle and brand the calves born after the earlier roundup. Spring roundup got under way when grass showed green, and might keep the riders working for as much as 40 days. The fall gather, starting near the beginning of September, generally lasted about a month. The camp above has been established at the edge of a small Montana town for the purpose of a roundup—probably in this case to collect young horses rather than cattle. The four cowboys at the right show the typical garb of the men in a roundup.

ON THE TRAIL

Charles Russell, one of the most competent painters of the Old West, called this scene *Laugh Kills Lonesome*. In the vast darkness of a night on the trail, talk and sleep were the only pastimes that existed.

The articles below were all part of the equipment that a cowboy used on the range: (1) rifle and rifle in holder, (2) spurs, (3) broad-brimmed hats, (4) catch rope or lariat, (5) branding irons, (6) six-shooter, belt, and holster, (7) boots, (8) saddles. The Mexicans had an old tradition of craftsmanship in leather and metals, and the more elaborately decorated items shown here are of Mexican design. When an American cowboy had money, he usually bought some Mexican gear.

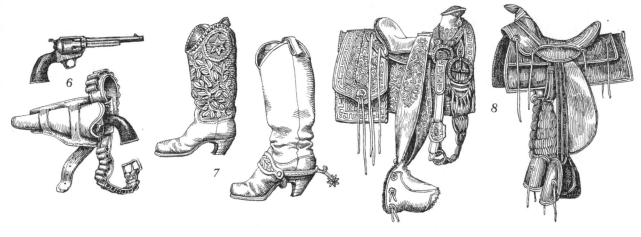

THE COWBOY AT WORK

Roping was often the most complicated part of a cowboy's job and required not only great skill with the use of the rope or lariat, but also expert horsemanship on the part of the cowboy. He had to perform highly involved operations while riding fast.

The cowboys worked the range in all kinds of weather, at all times of the day. The hands above gather around the fire at the back of a chuck wagon in the dead of winter. In the Russell painting below, cowboys break camp at dawn to begin a long day's work.

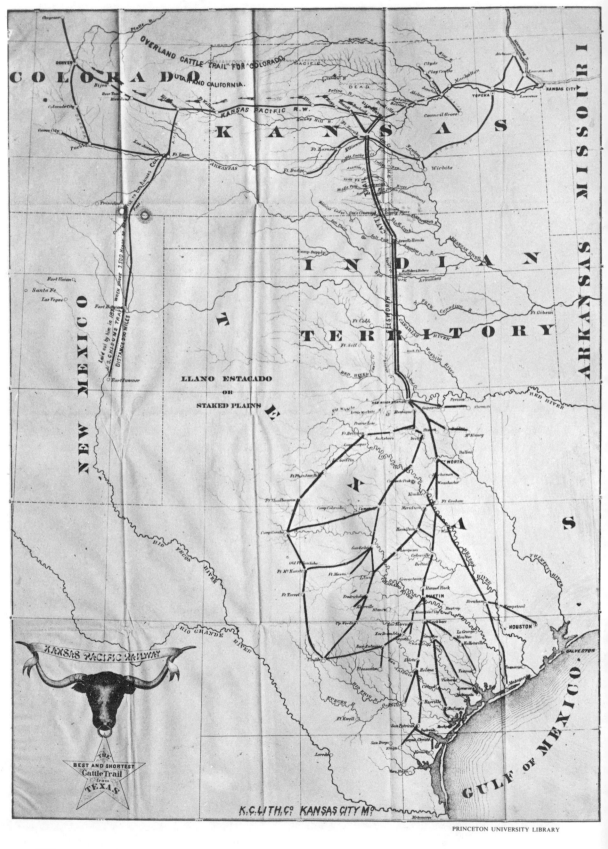

THE CATTLE DRIVES

UNIVERSITY OF TEXAS

The herd (above) is on the trail with cowboys riding behind it and on its flanks. They had to be on the alert for stray steers, which could easily start a stampede.

The Kansas Pacific Railway issued the map at the left in 1875 to persuade the cattlemen to use its line for shipping their stock. The smaller cattle trails run north to stops on the same railroad line.

Outlaws were another great danger to the cattle drivers. In the drawing at the right, one man stampedes a herd while three other outlaws tie up and beat the driver.

OVERLEAF: The cowboys in this Frederic Remington painting are defending their water hole against attacking Indians.

MUSEUM OF FINE ARTS OF HOUSTON

NEW YORK PUBLIC LIBRARY

751

Frederic Remington

THE COW TOWNS

The trail boss at the left is bargaining with a brave for permission to take his herd across Indian territory. For this privilege, the Indians often demanded tolls based on the size of the herd. There was little argument possible, for the ranchers did not want to risk their lives or cattle.

At the end of the cattle trails were cow towns like Dodge City, Kansas, shown (below, right) in 1878. Here herds were sold and shipped east on the railroad. In the woodcut (below, left), cattle are driven down the main street of Dodge City by cowboys, who are eager to finish their job.

KANSAS STATE HISTORICAL SOCIETY

COWBOYS HIT TOWN

WYOMING STATE ARCHIVES AND HISTORICAL DEPARTMENT

When the cowboys got to the end of the trails, they were paid off as soon as the herd was sold, and usually took a rest before starting the trip home. They had a lot of money to spend and a lot of time in which to spend it. Gambling (above) was one means of consuming both time and money. The group at the left has put some of their cash into fancy clothes, long watch chains, and new catch ropes—as well as into the photograph itself; which, as the figure on the left indicates, was posed with a sense of humor, probably to amuse their families at home. The scene at the right presents more of what the cowboy has come to mean today. These four have decided that they have been cheated at cards and are storming the gambling house, horses and all, where the deed was done. Such incidents were not infrequent, but they were not as common as the modern movies and television indicate. The painting is by Charles Russell.

758

CHAPTER 26

CATTLEMEN AND HOMESTEADERS

During the years in which legions of miners crawled antlike across the West, there were other important frontiers in the making. Forty-niners and their cousins the fifty-niners had dreaded the thought of crossing the Great American Desert to reach the mine fields, but as is so often the case, the anticipation proved worse than the reality. The desert, grim and forbidding, contained hidden resources, and draft animals not only survived on the dry, parched bunch grass in the summer, but to the amazement of many a newcomer they managed to live through the long, severe Western winters. Miners also discovered that beef cattle could be driven long distances, and after fattening in some grassy meadow near the trail's end, they were ready for conversion into steaks. In a land where transportation costs were high, this was valuable information, and more than one cattleman got his start selling beef to the prospectors.

Stock raising was already a well-

Two cowboys fire their guns into the air trying to stampede the herd out of the deep ravine into which it has wandered.

established American agricultural enterprise, but it was the existence of a vast area of open range west of the Mississippi River and the demands of an expanding population in the years following the Civil War that set the scene for what has been called the day of the cattleman. Since the 1830s, enormous herds had roamed the Southern plains, especially in Texas, and in the following decade some attempts were made to drive the animals to markets in both Missouri and California, and later all the way to Chicago. These sporadic early drives did little more than give a preview of what lay ahead, however, and they barely touched the vast resources of rapidly growing herds. The figures for 1850, which gave Texas about 330,000 head of cattle, and for 1860, which gave that state over 3,500,000 head, indicate what was happening. This tenfold increase drove down prices until cattle were nearly worthless in Texas. The Civil War cut off the Northern market, and when the Mississippi River was closed in mid-1863, a large portion of the Southwest was isolated from the Confederacy, too.

At the war's end, there were thou-

In the days of the beef bonanza and the range wars, the Texas plains at times resembled battlefields. Frederic Remington has painted what sometimes happened when armed cowboys from rival ranches fought over the ownership of disputed grazing lands.

sands of cattle to be seen on the plains of Texas, many of them with no brand or any other sign of identification. They became known as mavericks, a term that had come into use before the war. The explanation usually given for its origin is that Samuel Maverick, an early Texas rancher, failed to brand all his cattle one year, and soon his neighbors were calling all unbranded cattle by his surname. These strays were eagerly hunted down, for there was a great deal of money to be made in cattle. Aside from mavericks, Texas cattle could be bought at $4 or $5 a head and sold for perhaps $40. All that stood between the $4 cow in Texas and the $40 one at the market was dusty distance, and the business of moving the herds north produced the first large group of "cowboys."

Cattle drives and cow towns

A good many men saw the possibilities of this new venture soon after Appomattox, but the embers of the conflict burned too long in the spring of 1865 to permit a northward drive to get started that year. A beginning was made in the following year, although it is estimated that few more than 250,000 head of cattle were moved that season. As with many new businesses, the early drives were plagued by compli-cations. The terrain over which the herds were to be taken was unfamiliar to the herders, and the Kansans and Missourians who had suffered heavily in the war from bushwhackers were hostile to this new invasion of their lands. Finally, there were the difficulties of developing a smooth working organization on the road. An inexperienced young cowboy expressed the feelings of many when he wrote of lost cattle, incessant rain, and a diet of bread and coffee, concluding with the remark, "Have *not* got the *Blues* but am in a *hel of a fix*."

The "long drives" got their real be-

ginning in 1867. An Illinois stockman named Joseph G. McCoy established his cattle yards at Abilene, Kansas, on the Kansas Pacific Railway, and during that summer some 35,000 head of Texas beef came his way. The financial returns from his early shipments eastward were disappointing, but McCoy stuck to his notion that the business would eventually pay off. The following year, he advertised so widely in Texas newspapers that Abilene became one of the best known of the early "cow towns." It was the prototype of many a trail's-end settlement that grew up later as the rails moved west and the cattle drives curved in that direction to find fresh forage. One of the latter towns, Dodge City, would be more famous for its violence, for by the time "Dodge" grew up, the boys had developed a lot of refinements in the art of hell-raising.

The shenanigans of the cow town were, however, only a brief and bizarre interlude in an otherwise serious business. Life on the trail, so monotonous that the days were telescoped into one long, dusty tableau, was characterized by constant concern over the safety of the herd. Red-eyed, bone-weary men remained fiddlestring-taut until the last cow was herded into the waiting pens at the railroad. Only then did the men feel they had earned the right to let go—and they did so with enthusiasm and even violence.

All sizes of herds were moved along the trails, but after some experimenting, it was generally agreed that 2,500 was the most manageable size. A dozen men, each supplied with a half-dozen horses, could control a herd of this size during the wearying days and nights, which were often shattered by sudden thunderstorms. The cowboys attempted to move a herd at the rate of only 10 to 15 miles a day, covering from 300 to 450 miles a month, but even at that pace, the animals lost weight on the drive. Costs of a cattle drive varied, but usually an owner paid around $500 a month, and expected to get his cattle from Texas clear up to Montana for under $2,000. A herd of normal size could be moved for less than $1 a head, and if the losses were small, the owner recovered his cost quickly in the return from his sales.

The drive soon became as organized and as routine as a drill-field maneuver. After the animals were given a road brand, they were put on the trail, where the real herding began. In the van rode the "point," or guide; about a quarter of the way back, on either side, came men riding the "swing";

The downpour of rain, with its thunder and lightning, has frightened the herd, and a cowboy tries to prevent a stampede.

closer to the rear, on either side, came the "flank"; and back in the dust-filled rear was the "drag," who gathered up the strays. The chuck wagon, loaded with cowboys' gear and with food, was driven by the cook, who moved out ahead looking for a suitable location to "noon." When he found it—perhaps a grass-lined stream or some shady spot—he prepared food, and after the men had eaten, they rested. Two hours were generally allotted to this midday stop, so that the cattle

762

might graze and water before resuming the long trudge northward.

The movement of large herds with all the attendant color and excitement made a picturesque sight. Ernest Osgood, the cattleman's historian, painted one of the best word pictures of trail driving: "In after years, the drive of the Texas men became little short of an American saga. To all those who saw that long line of Texas cattle come up over a rise in the prairie, nostrils wide for the smell of wa-ter, dust-caked and gaunt, so ready to break from the nervous control of the riders strung out along the flanks of the herd, there came the feeling that in this spectacle there was something elemental, something resistless, something perfectly in keeping with the unconquered land about them."

Rise of the cattle kingdom

Not all cattlemen were content merely to drive their stock to the nearest railhead for immediate ship-

ment and sale. Experience proved that the cold, barren-looking land to the north was more habitable than it appeared, and animals could live through a normal winter there with little difficulty. The vast public domain was an ideal place to fatten cattle at no extra cost to the owner. By the 1870s, word of this "beef bonanza" had spread across the country and had found its way beyond the Atlantic into European financial circles. Reports that cattle increased in value as much as $10 a year, at a maintenance cost of perhaps only $1, excited the curiosity of New Yorkers and Londoners alike, but many were skeptical about these tales of fortunes being made on the open range. Agriculture had never been known as an occupation that made men wealthy, and in a day when oil and steel were beginning to produce millionaires, it sounded strangely out of tune with dominating economic themes to hear of poor herdsmen becoming men of means in a decade. Yet it was hard to ignore stories of 20%, 30%, and even 40% profits from free grass. Cautious Britons dug down and more

764

Wagons with watertight bodies ford the South Platte River at an Indian encampment in a vast panorama painted by William H. Jackson in 1866. A wagon might be pulled by 20 or more oxen.

than matched the wise money of New York to cash in on this latest Western boom. Some went west and entered the business directly; others simply loaned their money at interest and farmed the money market. Under favorable circumstances both groups of men profited.

John W. Iliff had a career rivaling the success stories of Horatio Alger, and his story is typical of many other Western "cattle kings." He came out to Colorado in 1859, along with many other youngsters who had gold in their eyes, only to find that placer mining was more than picking up nuggets from the ground. By raising vegetables for sale to miners, he made a modest stake—enough to buy a little store near Cheyenne, where he traded with passing immigrants. Exchanging groceries for footsore cattle at a favorable rate, he built the nucleus of a herd that soon grew enormously. When the railroad workers appeared,

Iliff was ready to sell beef in quantity, and to keep up his inventory, he made careful purchases from trail-driving outfits that passed his way. In 1878, when he died, this industrious ex-miner controlled miles of land along the South Platte River and owned around 35,000 head of cattle. Young men in the East intent on watching the captains of industry operate may have paused to consider the expanding economy of the West as a place to make their mark.

Montana growers, who waited a long time for their railroad, took advantage of the rich grassland in the territory and raised cattle so cheaply that they could afford to drive them all the way down to the Union Pacific's stock pens at Omaha. The miners led the way into Montana's mountains, but it was the ranchers who proved that the eastern flatlands could also be profitable. Railroads, eager to build west, saw an immediate source of income in the great herds of cattle to be shipped eastward, and they hastened to extend their lines to meet the trade. The ranchers also helped to prove that the flatlands were not the Great American Desert in any sense of the word, and that under favorable conditions crops would grow there. Many a ranch had its vegetable garden, and some ranchers even raised modest quantities of fodder. This was

766

The main street of a cow town, often littered with playing cards and bottles as evidence of its chief pastimes, was likely to see violence break out night or day.

ulus to corn production encouraged the development of cultivation techniques and the invention of new farm machinery. Farming on a larger scale in turn helped to create a demand for the increased manufacture of farm implements. Paralleling this development were the amazing growth of meat packing and the emergence of such names as Armour, Cudahy, Swift, and Hormel. Closer to its source, the cattle industry had considerable influence upon Western politics, and in such states as Colorado, Wyoming, and Montana, cattlemen's associations matched the power shown farther east by big business.

The cowpoke rides again

In a less tangible way, the industry left a deep mark upon a growing American folklore. The cowboy replaced earlier heroes, taking his place as the central figure in countless Westerns—first in dime novels, then in motion pictures, next on radio, and then in television programs. This weather-beaten, wiry, whipcord-tough individual—short on book learning and long on savvy—represented *the* American character to millions as he fought for what he thought was right, against all that was evil. He epitomized the sterling qualities of self-reliance, bravery, and resourcefulness, and became an idol to boys who would

all the encouragement the homesteader needed. With it, he was ready to invade the West himself.

As the cattle kingdom spread, its significance to American economic and social life became increasingly apparent. The attractions of ranching proved irresistible to many a Civil War veteran who wanted a new start in life after a long and bitter war. Added to this new source of manpower was capital, foreign and domestic, in ever larger quantities. Heavy investments on the high plains made today's Midwest a "feeder" area, where Western cattle fattened on Iowa or Nebraska corn as they were readied for packing houses. This stim-

A nester was a rancher who attempted to make a place for himself with a small cabin and corral in the country that originally belonged to big cattlemen.

never get near enough to horses to ride and only in this way could share in the excitement of the Old West.

The sodbusters' West

The stockmen and the cowboys proved to be only another advance guard in an invasion that was to conquer a domain stretching untouched for hundreds of miles. Unwittingly, these pioneers set the stage for a subsequent and bigger wave of newcomers known to them as sodbusters, grangers, or just plain homesteaders. The success of the ranchers, followed by the railroads and the tiny towns that sprang up alongside, pointed the way to thousands of more timid tillers of the soil who had stood back in the security of safer and more comfortable areas east of the Mississippi River. They edged forward, and were surprised to find that the "desert" did not burn them out. Then they ventured a little farther; still nothing drastic happened. Crops grew, and soon the railroads were hauling them away for sale. With this discovery, the rush was on, and in numbers that dwarfed all previous frontiers—those of the fur trapper, the miner, and the cattleman.

The movement was a long time coming. During the 1840s and 1850s, when the Mississippi Valley was absorbing a large part of the westward-moving agrarian invasion, there was little inclination to move beyond it. The desert theory, long accepted, persisted into the 1870s, and many a prospective settler was convinced that land west of the 100th meridian was good for nothing but chasing Indians. Even had they been persuaded differently, their reluctance to move would not have been greatly affected, for the desert country lacked the transportation necessary to a cash-crop economy. During the 1850s, there were no railroads beyond the Missouri River, except for minute beginnings in faraway California. The Civil War temporarily halted efforts to build a major transcontinental line. Western rivers —even the long and snakelike Missouri—offered little promise as practical routes to a market. The farmer's frontier, the traditional leader in the advance, was stalled until these barriers were gone. By the 1860s, farmers were considering a new move; by the 1870s, they were again on the march; in the 1880s, their invasion reached floodtide proportions.

Land without lumber

The first positive steps toward the removal of barriers on the plains came during the Civil War with the passage of the Homestead Act and the chartering of a transcontinental railroad, both in 1862. After Appomattox, thousands of veterans applied for the 160 acres of free land offered by the government, and despite the threat of Indian violence, the fear of vast distances, and even the opposition of well-entrenched cattle barons, the new agrarians marched westward.

What they found was no land of milk and honey. Their pleasure at

The farmer in the 1850s was considered the economy's backbone.

seeing vast expanses of countryside that would yield to the plow without the backbreaking, never-ending toil of clearing timber was dimmed by the realization that they would miss their old enemy, the tree. What would the farmer use to build his home and how would he heat it? The prairie offered few answers. Along some streams were soft cottonwood trees from which log cabins could be made, but the wood deteriorated rapidly and it made poor fuel. The man who found a stand of cottonwood trees was better off than his neighbor who found none at all and who had no recourse but to strip sod from the earth and pile it together into a rude sod house, or soddy. Where there was not so much as a nearby grove of willows, a substitute fuel was found in the dry dung, or "chips," left by herds of buffalo. The plains farmers and their children soon learned to carry small sacks with them as they went about the neighboring country and to husband each chip found, no matter how small. The cattle drives that passed through also contributed to the precious store of winter fuel—an inventory that was supplemented by dried sunflowers and even hay, wrapped tightly into "haycats."

Fuel, plentiful on earlier frontiers, was only one commodity in short supply in this new land. Water was equally precious. As historian Walter Webb remarked in his book *The Great Plains,* the pioneers' civilization "had stood on three legs—land, water, and timber; west of the Mississippi not one but two of these legs were withdrawn—water and timber—and civilization was left on one leg—land. It is small wonder that it toppled over in temporary failure." Although water was not easily available for irrigation, most farmers and ranchers could find enough for themselves and for their livestock by digging. Toward the end of the 1870s, the windmill became a relatively common sight in the West as the newcomers took advantage of a constant natural phenomenon—wind —to pump water. At first the device was a crude wooden structure, but when manufacturers realized the size of the potential market, thousands of metal windmills were sold on the plains. So the frontiersmen used their ingenuity by burning chips when they had no timber and by digging for water when they had no streams. "On the plains," Professor Webb quotes someone as saying, "the wind draws the water and the cows cut the wood."

Barbed wire changes the West

The sea of grass, as the endless plains were so often referred to, posed yet another problem—one that for a time seemed insoluble. Older and smaller farms east of the Mississippi River could be marked off with stone or split-rail fences, but in the new country, acreages were larger and fencing materials almost nonexistent. Until farmers could protect their crops from stray cattle, wandering buffalo herds, or other animals, there was not much profit in planting. The answer was provided by three men— Joseph Glidden, Jacob Haish, and Isaac Ellwood—all of whom played a part in the development of barbed wire. The story of this invention centers around Glidden, who tried to keep dogs out of his wife's flower bed by putting up a wire barrier. When his fence failed to keep the dogs out, Glidden hooked on a few sharp barbs, and to prevent these from sliding along the wire, he twisted two strands of it together, producing what soon became known as barbed wire. About the same time, Haish and Ellwood (who knew Glidden) developed a similar fence. Manufacture of the new fencing material began in 1874, and in that year about 10,000 pounds of it

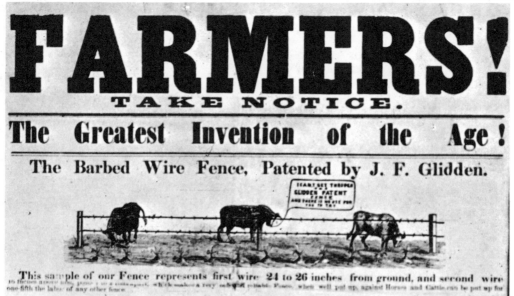

A poster issued in 1874 told farmers about the barbed wire that was to enclose the West. The men below are ranchers who have come to what they thought were public lands only to discover the wire. Masked, they are willing to be photographed as they break the fence with their crossed-stick "clippers".

*A homesteader and his family in Nebraska in 1886 present the strong face
of the early pioneer who lived in "sod-brick" huts on the treeless plains.*

were sold—a figure that became 80,-000 annually by the end of that decade. The earliest wire sold for around $20 a hundredweight. A tremendous demand for it led to mass production, and as better manufacturing methods were developed, the cost dropped to $1.80 a hundred within 25 years. Repeating rifles and revolvers are often thought of as revolutionizing Western life, but barbed wire may well have had a much deeper influence.

Tall stories and grasshoppers

Man's ingenuity might supply barbed wire as an answer to a perplexing agricultural problem, but there were other Western conditions that were not so readily met. Howling blizzards and sub-zero winter temperatures held the land in an icy grip for months, and spring brought floods rather than relief. Too often crops wilted in the searing summers. If the American sense of humor is based upon exaggeration and grim subjects, it must have been born on the frontier. Out on the plains, nature's exaggerations—temperature, wind, and rain or the lack of it—were so great that only the pioneer's ability to joke about them preserved his mental stability. Kansans told one another that when local sinners died during the summer, they were buried with their overcoats because hell would be colder. Fred Shannon, the agricultural historian, told a story about a mule that was supposed to have stood under a broiling sun, in a field of popcorn, until he was knee-deep in popped corn. Thinking the white stuff was snow, the mule froze to death.

Besides hot winds that shriveled plants and blew away precious topsoil, there were grasshoppers. From 1874 to 1876, they spread from Dakota Territory southward to Texas and westward to Colorado. They came in clouds thick enough to obscure the sun, eating first the tender green spears that peered through the topsoil and next assaulting trees and then plow handles or wagon sideboards that were even slightly greasy. Railroad tracks were so thoroughly covered with locusts that locomotives spun their wheels helplessly on only the slightest gradient. As if it were not bad enough to watch crops disappear, farmers stood by and saw chickens and turkeys eat themselves to death

on this heaven-sent banquet of insects.

Despite these adversities, the great agricultural invasion pressed forward; for every homesteader who failed, there always seemed to be two or three newcomers to take his place, profiting by the experience of his failure. The succeeding waves of homesteaders were learning how to adapt old methods of cultivation to this new land. They also learned rather quickly that the 160 acres of free land offered under the Homestead Act was often inadequate. Beyond the 100th meridian, where rainfall was light, it took more acreage to support a family than it did east of the Mississippi.

Free-soil legislation

In recognition of this fact and because of the increasing depletion of national timber resources, Congress passed the Timber Culture Act of 1873. Under its terms, homesteaders

Roof-deep blizzards often marooned farmers in flat whiteness, but the water stored in the ground from the melted snow helped crops flourish all summer.

Sod is being broken and turned by a homesteader and his great yoked oxen on land over which buffalo once grazed. Their scattered bones are plowed into the soil.

could obtain an additional 160 acres of free land from the government by planting a prescribed number of trees. It was thought that a tree belt would cut down the destruction of the wind, and many people still believed the old theory that wooded areas draw more rainfall. The law, however, was also an invitation to land speculation, and in 1891 it was repealed.

Further demands for modification of the Homestead Act resulted in passage of the Desert Land Act of 1877. Its title suggests awareness by Congress of the irrigation problem many Western farmers were complaining about as well as the persistent concept of the West as the Great American Desert. It applied to states generally west of the 100th meridian and stipulated that any settler could buy 640 acres of land if he would irrigate it within three years. The buyer was obliged to pay 25¢ per acre down, and upon complying with the act, he could buy the land for $1 more per acre. It was a classic case of Congressional bungling, and its failure was inevitable. Congress was trying to sell for $1.25 an acre of desert land that no homesteader would claim at a time when better land was available for nothing under the Homestead and Timber Culture Acts. The loose term "irrigate" was an invitation to fraud —one that was willingly accepted by

stockmen who simply doused a cup of water on 640 acres and called them irrigated. In 1884, land was being taken up at the rate of 500,000 acres a year, but only a small percentage of it was being patented in the names of the occupants. That is, stockmen fulfilled the initial requirements, grazed their stock on the land, and then made no final payment. The Desert Land Act was also impractical because it ignored the fact that large-scale irrigation was far too expensive for the typical homesteader.

Most of the legislation concerning Western land made the major mistake

of stipulating only the minimum that could be acquired under its terms. By failing to set a maximum, the laws allowed cattlemen to put together empires and made it easy for land speculators to make fortunes. The humble farmer, supposedly the beneficiary of such legislation, lost out to these more powerful forces.

Epitaph for the Old West

This last frontier movement, so often regarded as one characterizing the entire westward sweep, was not the traditional English-speaking advance of old. Whole armies of German, Norwegian, Swedish, and Russian immigrants came to till the soil. By the 1890s, there were over 400 towns in Minnesota with Swedish names, and in some Dakota communities Norwegian was the most common language.

These new pioneers, whether directly from Europe or from the East, differed in another way. They came west with no expectation of having to defend themselves against the violence of earlier frontiers. The late 19th-century settlers felt no necessity to carry rifles; it was the government's duty to protect them. That attitude alone was

775

enough to demonstrate the passing of the frontier.

The homesteaders usually came by rail, although some continued to travel by covered wagons. After the Union Pacific and Central Pacific Railroads were linked at Promontory Summit, Utah, in 1869, a network of Western railroads was built. In 1870, the Kansas Pacific reached Denver, and one of its employees, General William J. Palmer, left that company to start his own Denver & Rio Grande Railway—a road that would run along the Rockies from Denver to El Paso and even to Mexico City. The Santa Fe—more properly the Atchison, Topeka & Santa Fe— grew, from a tiny road chartered by Cyrus Holliday in 1859 to run between two Kansas towns, into a transcontinental system. By the 1880s, its trains were running from the Missouri River to Los Angeles.

Across the Northern plains stretched the Chicago, Burlington & Quincy, the Chicago, Milwaukee & St. Paul, the Northern Pacific, and the Great Northern. These, and the railroads already mentioned, were normally built with land-grant subsidies—except for the Great Northern. This line, conceived by the "one-eyed man of vision," Jim Hill, struggled across Minnesota, into Dakota, and westward to the coast without such help from the government. Not only did Hill succeed, but before he was through, he had (with the aid of J. P. Morgan) bought up the Burlington line before a surprised E. H. Harriman could act. (For a closer look, see *The Legend of Jim Hill* at the end of this volume.) These lines and many others covered the West like a giant iron spider web, serving existing communities, creating their own little towns, and contributing to the growth of a whole new and great agricultural domain.

On July 12, 1893, a young history professor from the University of Wisconsin named Frederick Jackson Turner read a scholarly paper to a group of historians assembled in Chicago for the Columbian Exposition. Basing his remarks on the 1890 census report, he noted that the frontier had ceased to exist. For a long time, areas having two or more people per square mile were regarded as settled; lands having less population were considered unsettled; and between the two areas had run an imaginary line separating the wilderness from civilization. The invasion of the sodbusters in the years following the Civil War had gradually erased this frontier line, leaving behind only isolated unsettled pockets.

Turner's paper was an epitaph for the Old West. "To the frontier," he said, "the American intellect owes its striking characteristics . . . coarseness and strength combined with acuteness and inquisitiveness; that practical, inventive turn of mind . . . that restless, nervous energy; that dominant individualism . . . and withal that buoyancy and exuberance that comes with freedom."

COLLECTION OF C. R. SMITH

THE LAST WARS
WITH THE INDIANS

When on July 18, 1881—with most of the famous Indian chiefs on reservations—Sitting Bull surrendered with his tribe at Fort Buford, North Dakota, the end had come for the Indian wars and for the Indian way of life. From then on, the great tribes that had retreated step by step from the white man, fighting furiously for their very existence, would fight no longer. Instead, they would live quietly in one place. But the last wars with the Indians were bloody and expressed all the desperation and anguish of a doomed man refusing to die. They gave to the Indian story some of its most famous names and victories.

CUT NOSE

LITTLE CROW

This painting was done on a barrelhead by Anton Gag.

MINNESOTA MASSACRE

The peace with the Indians in Minnesota was broken on August 17, 1862, when the Santee Sioux under Little Crow began a six-week massacre of the white man. The settlers made a valiant effort to defend themselves (below, left), but the attacks of braves like Cut Nose killed even women and children without hesitation before Colonel Henry H. Sibley (right) regrouped his forces and defeated Little Crow's men. A military commission condemned 306, but President Lincoln commuted the death sentence of all but 38, who were hanged in public in Mankato, Minnesota (below).

SIBLEY COUNTY HISTORICAL SOCIETY, MINNESOTA

MINNESOTA HISTORICAL SOCIETY

THE LAST WARS WITH THE INDIANS

THE GREAT DISGRACE

The end of the Civil War brought all-out war to the Plains Indians. Soldiers freed from the Eastern battlefields after Appomattox were sent west under battle-trained officers. They went there to protect civilians, so they could build homes and farms peacefully on the frontier, and to make sure they could travel westward in safety. But the presence of the soldiers and the increased traffic on the hunting grounds led only to fighting. Much of what took place was a disgrace to the white man.

780

One of the worst Indian incidents involved Chiefs Black Kettle and White Antelope (seated third and fourth from the left in the photograph opposite). They were promised by Major E. W. Wynkoop (left front, in hat), commandant at Fort Lyon, Colorado, that they could live in peace in the Sand Creek area, 30 miles from the fort. Wynkoop was replaced and his promise was broken. Under the command of a former minister, Colonel J. M. Chivington (right), some 600 state militiamen attacked on November 29, 1864. The picture below shows what the Colorado volunteers did to more than 700 Indians, most of whom were women and children and all of whom were unprepared for any such onslaught because they had been assured of peace. Chief White Antelope died at once, but Chief Black Kettle escaped to the south to tell other tribes of the white man's treachery.

VICTORY
AND
DEATH

Red Cloud, shown with his great-grand-
daughter Burning Heart, was an Oglala
Sioux who had both victory and defeat in
his fight against the white man. Near Fort
Phil Kearny he killed Captain William J.
Fetterman and more than 80 men in an
attack after an ambush, but less than a
year later, in August, 1867, he lost 200 men
in what is now called the Wagon Box battle.

Roman Nose (right), a Northern Cheyenne, six feet, three inches tall and weighing 230 pounds, earned the reputation in his tribe—as a result of skill in battle—of being bulletproof. His death occurred during the Beecher Island fight. Here cavalrymen had repeating rifles and Colt revolvers, and in the attacks on the morning of September 17, 1868, they were able to hold off the Indians. Up to this time, Roman Nose had not gone into battle because his war medicine warned of his death. Finally he decided to fight and was shot almost at once as he rode through the cavalrymen, who had taken cover behind horses (below).

CUSTER
COMES
WEST

Glory-hunting George A. Custer was a hero of the Civil War when he arrived on the southern plains to help clean up the Indian raiders. On November 26, 1868, he attacked Black Kettle's band, which had camped on the Washita River in the present state of Oklahoma. Despite the treachery he had met with at Sand Creek, Black Kettle wanted peace with the white man, but Custer did not accept it, and his surprise attack (left) killed more than 100 Cheyennes. It was Chief Sitting Bull (top, left, with his rifle below the portrait) who got revenge on Custer at Little Big Horn when all of the American force was massacred. At the right is a picture of Custer; above is a meeting between Sitting Bull and Colonel Nelson A. Miles, who was instructed to get him onto a reservation.

THE LAST WARS WITH THE INDIANS

CUSTER'S LAST STAND

There is no exact record of what took place at Little Big Horn when all of Custer's men were defeated, for no white man lived to tell what he saw. W. R. Leigh's painting is not accurate as to terrain, saddles, and many other features, but it does capture the fury of the massive Indian attack that lasted no more than an hour but killed more than 250 American cavalrymen.

GERONIMO

After Sitting Bull's surrender, the main force went out of the Indians' fight for their way of life, and most of them retired to reservations. Geronimo (left), a chief of the Apaches, was the last of the great Indian fighters to refuse to give up. He was pursued into Mexico, where he finally surrendered in 1886, and is shown (below, right) in custody at Fort Bowie, Arizona, in September of that year. But the image of the American Indian did not die with him. At the right is a 1907 painting by Carl Hassman, expressing all the excitment and color the Indian has given to the American legend of the great West.

CHAPTER 27

TAMING THE WILD WEST

America's last frontier spanned only 30 years, roughly from the Colorado gold rush of 1859 to the admission into the Union of the six "Omnibus States"—Washington, Montana, the two Dakotas, Wyoming, and Idaho—in 1889 and 1890. It was the miners and the cattlemen, the railroad builders and the homesteaders who really conquered it, but today it is the United States cavalry that is best remembered as the conqueror.

Into these 30 years were crowded some of the fiercest and most desperate battles in the long undeclared war that white men had been waging against the Indians ever since setting foot on the continent almost four centuries earlier. The Indians of the plains were the last to submit to the advancing wave of white civilization. Today, nearly 75 years after their final defeat, we think of these Indians— with their long feathered war bonnets, their conical tepees, their superb horsemanship, their swift and sudden raids on covered-wagon caravans,

As the white man advanced, the Indians kept migrating west to new lands until, finally, there was nowhere for them to go.

their duels with blue-clad soldiers— as typical of all American tribes.

Before the Civil War, there had been a number of isolated clashes between the Plains Indians and white men passing through their territory; and during the war, the Sioux of Minnesota had gone on the rampage, massacring some 400 whites. About all the United States Army could do in these years was fight a defensive war, guarding the trails, protecting settlements, punishing Indians like the Minnesota Sioux for their crimes. A good part of the army's work was simply keeping peace among the rival tribes, for these Indians almost lived for intertribal warfare. Only after the Civil War did the victorious North, its troops free for duty on the frontier, launch a grand offensive designed to conquer the Indians and tame the West. Before this was done, however, the army had fought more than 1,000 battles with Indians, and 2,571 white men—both soldiers and civilians— had been killed. No one will ever know exactly how many Indians died, but the number is estimated at 5,500.

The Indians who tried to live in peace with the white man were often met with deceit and treachery, as Black Kettle, a chief of the Southern Cheyennes of eastern Colorado, found out in 1864. Promised the protection of the army if his people lived in peace, Black Kettle narrowly escaped with his life when volunteers surrounded his village on Sand Creek and massacred, without warning, 300 of the Indians living there. Quite naturally, the Indians sought revenge.

Moving north in the winter of 1864, the remnants of the Southern Cheyennes attacked stagecoaches, raided white settlements, killed cattle, and even chopped down the telegraph poles that symbolized the white invasion of their territory. In the spring of 1865, they joined the Sioux, the Northern Cheyennes, and the Arapahoes in the Powder River country of northeastern Wyoming. Once Black Kettle's story had been heard, members of these other tribes swore to join in warfare against the whites. Among the chiefs who pledged their aid were some soon to be famous—Red Cloud, Sitting Bull, Old-Man-Afraid-of-His-Horses, Crazy Horse.

The United States sent General Pattrick Edward Connor out to round up these Indians in the spring of 1865, but with bad maps, poor guides, and insufficient provisions, Connor's expedition failed. Next the government sent a peace commission west. The commissioners granted the Sioux, Cheyennes, and Arapahoes the right to remain in the Powder River country that was already theirs, asking only that the government be permitted to build forts along the Bozeman Trail, a short cut to the Montana gold fields. No important chief signed this treaty, but nevertheless the government went ahead with its plans.

In the summer of 1866, Colonel Henry B. Carrington arrived at Fort Laramie with several hundred infantrymen. At the very moment that peace commissioners were telling Indian chiefs gathered at the fort that the United States was not interested in the Powder River country, Colonel Carrington announced that he was going to build the forts along the Bozeman Trail. That summer Carrington enlarged an existing post at the head of the Powder River and named it Fort Reno, built Fort Phil Kearny between two forks of Piney Creek a little farther north, and opened a third post, Fort C. F. Smith, just across the present state line of Montana.

Although Carrington claimed that the Bozeman Trail was now adequately protected, the three forts remained under a virtual siege for the next two years. The Indians kept a constant watch on the invaders, waiting for a chance to strike at isolated and unprotected groups of soldiers.

On the morning of December 21, 1866, lookouts at Fort Phil Kearny received distress signals from a detail of men sent out to chop wood in the surrounding hills. Reluctantly, Colonel Carrington let a boastful young officer, Captain William J. Fetterman,

At the Wagon Box battle in 1867, the cavalry, protected by a circle of wagons and using rifles that reloaded automatically, defeated the attacking Indians.

lead the rescue party. A West Point graduate, Fetterman had previously announced to fellow officers that, with 80 men, he could ride through the entire Sioux nation. That day, Fetterman had his 80 men, and the Indians let him ride through their midst—for a little while. But it was an ambush, and the Indians soon closed in to slaughter Fetterman's entire group.

Shortly after the Fetterman massacre, the onslaught of winter brought temporary relief from Indian raids. But the following summer, Red Cloud attempted to repeat the earlier Sioux success. On August 2, 1867, he sent nearly 1,000 warriors to attack a wood train. This time, however, the soldiers were armed with new breech-loading rifles. Instead of pursuing decoys into an ambush, the soldiers made a circle of the wagon boxes and waited for the Indians to attack them. Surprised by

the rapid fire from the wagon boxes, the Indians lost 200 men in dead and wounded—to five white casualties.

Although the Wagon Box battle was considered a revenge for the Fetterman massacre, it did not mean an end to troubles along the Bozeman Trail. A year later, in 1868, the three forts were abandoned, and the Indians once more roamed freely in the Powder River country. That year the railroad had reached Wyoming, and it was becoming cheaper and less dangerous to ship and travel by rail to Utah and then north into Montana than it was to follow the Bozeman Trail through hostile Indian territory.

Custer goes to the plains

The year that the army withdrew from the Bozeman Trail saw the debut of the most spectacular cavalry officer of the Indian wars. Despite the treach-

The Cheyenne Indians, seeking to stop the advance of railroads through their ancestral hunting grounds in Kansas in 1867, tear up the rails and burn the ties. The railroad brought the settlers and white hunters, who disturbed and killed off the Indian's migrating herds of buffalo.

ery of the Sand Creek massacre, Chief Black Kettle of the Southern Cheyennes had tried to keep the peace with the white man. By the fall of 1868, he had led his people to an encampment on the Washita River in the Indian Territory (present-day Oklahoma). While Black Kettle was peacefully seeking permission from army authorities to move his village closer to Fort Cobb, two Cheyenne war parties, fresh from raids against white settlements in Kansas, arrived at the Washita. Instructed to punish these hostile Indians, a handsome young Civil War veteran, Lieutenant Colonel George A. Custer, instead surprised Black Kettle's peaceful village with a morning raid on November 26, 1868. This time Black Kettle paid with his life for trusting the white man.

There were many such treacherous attacks by whites upon Indians, and there were instances in which the Indians were the aggressors. But

whether they were attacking whites or merely defending themselves, the tribesmen fought with cunning, bravery, and sometimes with cruelty. They knew their very existence depended on the outcome of this final struggle.

The plains and hills of this last frontier were undergoing an enormous change. The wide open spaces were being filled up with farms and villages and then towns; soon railroads and telegraph lines linked these settlements. Indians learned that telegraph lines could carry messages that would bring soldiers to trouble spots quickly, and put this knowledge to use: Before

attacking, they often cut the wires.

The railroad was another threat to the old way of life. It not only brought white settlers west, but it also brought hunters and sportsmen to shoot the buffalo that was the Indian's mainstay. The Indians had used all parts of the buffalo—meat for food, hide for clothing and shelter, bones for tools and weapons. The white hunters often shot just for fun, leaving so many carcasses where they fell that in places the plains were white with bleached bones. In 1850, there had been an estimated 15,000,000 buffalo on the plains; 35 years later, they were virtually extinct.

Slaughtering the buffalo, General Phil Sheridan once said, amounted to destroying the Indians' commissary.

Indian wars on the northern plains

The gold rush into the Black Hills of South Dakota and Wyoming in 1874 brought a climax to the Indian wars on the northern plains. The Indians had seen other gold rushes and knew that the coming of the miners was just the beginning of a total invasion. This was sacred territory to the Sioux and to their allies, the Cheyennes and Arapahoes, and since the abandonment of the Bozeman Trail in 1868, they had lived there in peace. In the summer of 1874, this peace was shattered when Custer led the Seventh Cavalry into the Black Hills, supposedly to test the soil for its gold content. His favorable report on mineral resources brought a stampede of miners that the government was powerless to halt. Sioux leaders, among them Sitting Bull and Crazy Horse, refused to sell their land and braced themselves for the fight they knew was coming.

In December, 1875, the government ordered all Indians in the area to move to reservations by January 31, 1876, or face military action. It is doubtful that the word reached Sitting Bull and Crazy Horse; even if it had, they would probably have ignored the order.

In March, the Indians repulsed an attack by Colonel J. J. Reynolds and the Third Cavalry on a Powder River village, and by June, Sitting Bull had gathered together 1,000 warriors. This force defeated General George Crook at the Rosebud River, and it looked as if the Indians might win the war. Encouraged by these initial successes, more Indians joined Sitting Bull, and the enlarged band moved to a new encampment on the banks of the Little Big Horn River, a name that was soon to become famous.

On the night of June 24, 1876, Custer and the elite Seventh Cavalry approached Sitting Bull's village on the Little Big Horn. The next morning, Custer divided his force and attacked. The resulting massacre of some 250 soldiers has been immortalized in story and pictures as Custer's Last Stand.

The defeat at the Little Big Horn shocked the nation. News reached the East on July 4, 1876, the 100th anniversary of the Declaration of Independence, and outraged Americans howled for revenge.

Colonel Nelson A. Miles was sent to pursue Sitting Bull, but the proud chief escaped to Canada. Crazy Horse surrendered voluntarily, and died in September, 1877. Four years later, on July 18, 1881, Sitting Bull, tired of exile and weary of fighting, surrendered at Fort Buford, North Dakota.

The white man conquers

While war was raging on the northern plains, Indians of the Southwest were also fighting for survival. Since the 1820s, the Kiowas and the Comanches had been raiding along the Santa Fe Trail. In 1867, however,

Fighting in northern California in the great lava beds, the Modoc Indians made a heroic, last-ditch stand against the oncoming white man in 1872–73.

many of the chiefs signed a treaty with the government, agreeing to settle on Texas and Oklahoma reservations. Quanah Parker, the half-breed son of a Comanche chief and a captive white woman, refused to sign the treaty and, in 1874, led a desperate last-ditch fight against the whites. Only when his war failed did Quanah Parker submit to being confined on a reservation.

The Navahos were subdued by Kit Carson and were removed to eastern New Mexico. But in 1868 the government let them return to their beloved mesas and canyons on the New Mexico-Arizona-Utah border where they have lived ever since. With a population of 176,000, they are today America's largest Indian tribe.

The neighboring Apaches were more warlike. Led by chiefs like Cochise and Mangas Coloradas, they resisted confinement on reservations until the early 1870s. Even after some had signed treaties with the whites, others continued the struggle for independence. The most famous and most elusive of the hostile Apaches was Geronimo. American troops pursued him into Mexico in one futile chase, and not until September, 1886, did he surrender. In 1903, the once-fierce fighter, now converted to Christianity, became a tourist attraction at the St. Louis World's Fair.

Indians west of the Rocky Mountains provided two of the most dramatic episodes of the last wars of the Indians. In 1872–73, the Modocs staged a dramatic fight to the finish in the lava caves of northern California. At one time, nearly 1,000 soldiers were besieging a band of 250 Indians that

797

Walking slowly toward the assembled cavalry officers, Joseph, the chief of the Nez Perce, accepts the honorable terms of surrender offered him in 1877.

included but 70 or 80 warriors. Only after field guns shelled their position did the Indians surrender. Their leader, Kintpuash—better known as Captain Jack—and three of his lieutenants were hanged.

In the spring of 1877, Chief Joseph of the Nez Perce reluctantly agreed to take his people from their homeland in the Wallowa Valley of eastern Oregon to a reservation. This land had been guaranteed to them forever by a treaty of 1855, but now white settlers were beginning to move in. Before the Nez Perce could leave, some of the whites stole several hundred of their horses. After living in peace for

72 years, the Nez Perce decided to go to war.

Realizing that the odds were against his band of 400 to 500, Chief Joseph attempted to lead them to safety in Canada. In the next four months, on a 1,000-mile trek that took the band within 30 miles of the Canadian border, he fought over a dozen battles with four different army columns sent to pursue him. Surrounded, freezing and starving, the Nez Perce gave up on October 5, 1877.

Chief Joseph's speech of surrender stands as the epitaph for all the defeated warriors of a proud race. "I am tired of fighting," he said. "My people ask me for food, and I have none to give. It is cold, and we have no blankets, no wood. My people are starving to death. Where is my little daughter? I do not know. Perhaps, even now, she is freezing to death. Hear me, my chiefs. I have fought; but from where the sun now stands, Joseph will fight no more." Drawing his blanket over his face to hide his shame, he walked into the army camp as a prisoner.

Wovoka prophesies a messiah

By 1881, then, most of the hostile Indians had been forced onto reservations. They now had nothing but their dreams, but even this led to trouble. In January, 1889, a Nevada Paiute named Wovoka had a vision about the coming of an Indian messiah. This savior, Wovoka said, would bring back the Indian dead; the buffalo would reappear and the white man would vanish. The Indians would once again rule the land. To speed the messiah's coming, Wovoka asked his disciples to perform a ritualistic dance.

The new Ghost Dance cult, as it was called, quickly spread across the West. Among the converts were Sitting Bull's Sioux, who had been living on reservations for the previous eight years. The government feared the dancers would rise up and attempted to suppress the Ghost Dance. It was in the midst of this renewed Indian excitement that the last tragic incident of the Indian wars occurred.

A band of Sioux was waiting to surrender at Wounded Knee Creek,

South Dakota, when someone fired; no one seems sure whether it was an Indian or a soldier. Training their rapid-firing guns on the Indians, the troopers spared neither man, woman, nor child. Later, soldiers returned to the scene of the massacre and gathered up 200 dead, frozen into grotesque shapes, and hurriedly buried them in a common pit.

"We were happy when he first came," an Indian chief once said of the white man. "We first thought he came from the Light; but he comes like the dark of evening now, not like the dawn of the morning. He comes like a day that has passed, and night enters our future with him."

The railroad brings peace

Most Americans at the time were glad to see the last of the Indian menace. Few realized the tragedy of their defeat. "We took away their country and their means of support, broke up their mode of living, their habits of life, introduced disease and decay among them," General Sheridan wrote sadly in 1878, "and it was for this and against this that they made war. Could anyone expect less?"

Most people today see the conclusion of the Indian wars as a triumph of the troopers who fought actions all across the West. The thunder of hoofs, the smell of sweaty horses, and the blare of bugles in the afternoon make exciting reading, but it was the coming of the homesteader, significantly by railroad car, that finally ended the

The Spirit of the Frontier, *painted in 1872 by John Gast, symbolizes the procession of American civilization west and the end (left) of the great open plains.*

nomadic way of life for the Plains Indian. The railroad, whether used as a weapon by the army to shuttle troops back and forth to trouble spots or as a means of bringing in homesteaders, became the principal instrument for pacifying the West. In 1880, General W. T. Sherman wrote that the presence of troops and settlers drastically reduced the danger from Indians, but he felt that even more important were the railroads. Three years later, as he prepared to retire, he reaffirmed this belief. "I regard the building of these railroads as the most important event of modern times," he said, "and believe that they account fully for the peace and good order which now prevail throughout the country, and for the extraordinary prosperity which now prevails in this land."

In many ways, the last Western frontier differed from earlier ones. Once the cattle rancher or the farmer had settled far out on the plains, relying upon transportation to provide a market for his goods, he became dependent upon both the market and the railroad. He tended to be a specialist, raising a cash crop. With income from it he bought the items that his forebears used to manufacture at home. A crop failure often meant the total loss of a year's income. When market prices fell, the Western farmer was as badly off as any Eastern manufacturer. Thus his generation felt the impact of depressions more severely than that of earlier farmers, and this fact was to be important to American history.

By the turn of the 20th century, life in the American West differed little from that in other parts of the country. Its political structure was al-

most completed. Only Oklahoma, New Mexico, and Arizona remained as territories in 1900, and within a dozen years they, too, would be states. By this time, law and order reached into the most remote spots, and only an occasional train robbery disturbed the peace. Western men and women thought increasingly in national terms, helped by newspapers carrying wire-service dispatches. Mail-order houses helped them look much like other Americans. The day of the automobile, motion picture, and radio was not far ahead, and these would complete the transition.

MAIN TEXT CONTINUES IN VOLUME 10

The Legend of Jim Hill

A SPECIAL CONTRIBUTION BY
STEWART H. HOLBROOK

When James J. Hill died in 1916, the New York Times *said of this master railroader of the Northwest, "Greatness became him, and was a condition of his errand here."*

Long before his death, some 70 years ago, Jim Hill had become a legend in the American West. James Jerome Hill, the Empire Builder, the man who *made* the Northwest, or who wrecked it—Jim Hill, the shaggy-headed, one-eyed old so-and-so of Western railroading.

In two of the best-remembered stories of Jim Hill, one shows him a hero, the other a villain. Once when a crew was trying to clear track for a Great Northern passenger train stalled in a blinding snowstorm, President Hill came out to snatch a shovel from a man and send him into the president's car for hot coffee, while Hill himself shoveled like a rotary plow. One after the other, the gandy-dancers drank fine Java while the Great Northern's creator faced the storm. *That* was Jim Hill. Again, because the mayor of a small Minnesota town objected, mildly, to all-night switching, Hill had the depot torn down and set up two miles away. That, too, was Jim Hill.

Hill began life with nothing. At the end he

Hill started in St. Paul with river steamers, then changed to railroads, and thus helped stimulate the great westward migration after the Civil War.

was lord of an empire that reached from the Great Lakes to Puget Sound, from the Canadian border to Missouri and Colorado. He had staked out provinces in China and Japan. He died worth $53,000,000, won in a region so sparsely settled that most Easterners believed it was a worthless wilderness.

Born in 1838 in Canada, Hill arrived at 18 in the raw new settlement at the head of navigation on the Mississippi that was beginning to dislike its pioneer name of Pig's Eye, and was calling itself St. Paul. The time was mid-1856. St. Paul was in its first notable boom. The prosperity was to last only 12 months longer before the panic of 1857 hit. But 12 months were all Hill needed. In that period he put down such firm roots that the city remained his home base for the next six decades.

His first job was on the St. Paul waterfront, where he clerked for an outfit running a line of packet steamers. By 1865, he had set up for himself as a forwarding agent, and a local daily paper observed that "J. J. Hill is now prepared to give shippers the lowest rates ever quoted from here to Eastern points. Mr. Hill has nearly all the important carriers of freight in his own hands."

Among the older businessmen observing Hill's career was Norman W. Kittson, acting as agent in St. Paul for the venerable Hudson's Bay Company. Previously, Kittson had acted for the independent trappers and traders, and he continued to do so, an arrangement that satisfied nobody. Kittson proposed that Hill devise a way to transport the independents and their various supplies from the United States

803

St. Paul, Minnesota, in 1856, the year James Hill arrived, had a population of fewer than 10,000 but was booming. It was to be the center of his operations for 60 years.

to the fur and farming regions of Canada.

The Hudson's Bay Company was operating what it considered a monopoly steamboat line on the Red River, which flowed north out of Dakota. Hill put a boat of his own on the Red. He added another. He had bonded his steamers, thus complying with a United States customs law that until then had been a dead letter. The Bay Company's vessels were suddenly barred from carrying freight, and until the Canadian firm could comply with the unobserved law, the Hill boats enjoyed a lucrative monopoly.

Hill promptly began a rate war against the Bay Company boats so effective as to cause Donald Smith, the company's governor, to visit St. Paul. The outcome was a coalition. Shipping rates on the Red went high and stayed high. During its first season, the Kittson-Hill combine returned a net profit of 80%.

While engaged in his now numerous activities, Hill watched the steady decay of the St. Paul & Pacific Railroad. If they could lay hands on that streak of rust and corruption, he told Kittson, it could be made profitable. But Hill and Kittson could muster only a few thousand dollars. To get a firm hold on the St. Paul & Pacific called for infinitely more money. Through Donald Smith and Smith's

cousin, George Stephen, head of the Bank of Montreal, $6,000,000 was raised. Hill and Kittson then borrowed and mortgaged, adding $780,000 to the syndicate. The four men took over the bankrupt company and reorganized it as the St. Paul, Minneapolis & Manitoba Railroad.

Hill was just 40 when he set out to make something out of the bankrupt line. Directing the job in person, he drove his construction crews at a furious rate. Across Minnesota went the rails, then north to the border to meet the Canadian Pacific, which built a line south from Winnipeg. Two thumping wheat harvests followed completion of the first Hill railroad; the freight traffic became immense. What had been a trickle of immigrants from Norway and Sweden turned to a flood, and not without reason: Hill's agents had been in Scandinavia singing the glories of the Red River of the North. Homesteads could be had free, or Hill would sell land still owned by the Manitoba Railroad, at $2.50 an acre.

Jim Hill's idea of a railroad was not a piece of track to connect the Twin Cities and Winnipeg. As early as 1879, he told his directors that he meant to push the line across the continent to Puget Sound. Some of his colleagues were alarmed. No one else had attempted to build a transcontinental railroad without a government subsidy. Even if by some chance Hill did manage to lay rails to Puget Sound, how could he compete with the old subsidized lines, the Northern Pacific and the Union Pacific? When his presumptuous plan became public, his railway was labeled Hill's Folly.

Hill's Folly moved westward with speed. Soon the main line started the long haul across Montana, running well north of the Northern Pacific, which Hill pretended to ignore, except to set his rates low in territory where he could compete.

Hill was ruthless. Near Great Falls, Montana, which Hill's Folly reached in 1887, he laid his rails in an arc clear around Fort Benton, whose shortsighted townsmen had rejected his demand for a right of way free of charge. This left the settlement a good mile from the tracks. Great Falls had been debating how much to charge Hill for a strip through the city, but observing what had occurred at Fort Benton, it presented him with a dandy right of way through the center of its city park.

At last the Great Northern reached Puget Sound at Everett, Washington, early in 1893. It was a bad year for railroads. The Santa Fe and the Union Pacific went into receivership. And, to the great delight of Hill, so did his major competitor, the Northern Pacific. Of all the railroads that reached the West Coast, only the Great Northern remained intact.

Hill had studied the failing Northern Pacific closely, and now he began buying its stock. The road was reorganized with the help of J. Pierpont Morgan and became, for all practical purposes, a second track for the Great Northern. The two roads became known as the Hill lines, and Hill was planning further expansion for them: He wanted nothing less than the great Midwestern property called the Chicago, Burlington & Quincy Railroad.

He wanted the Burlington because it would give him entry to Chicago and St. Louis. It touched the Great Northern at St. Paul and the Northern Pacific at Billings, Montana. Then, too, the Burlington would give Hill a connection with the cotton-hauling roads entering St. Louis and Kansas City, and with the smelters of Colorado and South Dakota, and the packing houses of Omaha. Hill and J. P. Morgan bought the Burlington from under the nose of Edward H. Harriman, who also wanted it.

Ten years younger than Hill, Harriman "looked like a bookkeeper," but he was also one of the few men who did not fear Morgan.

Photographed just before his death in 1916, the harsh yet penetrating and sensitive face of Hill reveals the qualities that made him successful.

Hill and his son Louis stand beside the six-foot wheat, grown on the Great Northern farmlands, to prove the abundance of their territory.

In fact, Harriman feared nobody. At 21 he had owned a seat on the New York Stock Exchange. He headed a syndicate to take over the foundering Union Pacific. (He was soon to get control of the Central Pacific and Southern Pacific as well.) Now he felt ready to begin what went into railroad history as the Hill-Harriman wars. Each man meant to dominate railroading in the Northwestern United States.

The Hill-Morgan coup—getting the Burlington—occurred in March, 1901. At almost the same time, Harriman, with the backing of Kuhn, Loeb & Company, New York bankers, started to buy secretly into the

Northern Pacific. If he couldn't get the Burlington, then he would try to control Hill's second road. The stock-buying was begun so astutely that neither Hill nor Morgan suspected what was going on. In fact, everything looked so serene in April that Morgan sailed for Europe while Hill set out to roll westward across his own empire.

Late in April, Hill, then in Seattle, noted a sharp rise in Northern Pacific shares. It troubled him because the Hill-Morgan group owned less than half of the road's stock. Usually a strong minority interest was enough to control a railroad, but not always. Hill acted quickly. He had his car hitched to a locomotive, ordered the tracks cleared, and started a fast run to Chicago, and then on to New York. He went immediately to the office of Jacob H. Schiff of Kuhn, Loeb and demanded to know if Schiff was buying Northern Pacific shares for Harriman. Yes, said Schiff, he was. What was more, if the Hill-Morgan group would not let Harriman have the Burlington, then Harriman was going to buy the Northern Pacific out from under them.

Hill went to the House of Morgan with the bad news. The partners cabled Morgan, asking for permission to buy 150,000 shares of Northern Pacific common stock. This happened on a Friday. The next day, while the Morgan partners awaited a reply, Harriman thought to play safe by buying another 40,000 shares. He called Schiff's office and gave the order. It was never executed. The devout Schiff was at the synagogue.

By Monday it was too late. Trading on the Exchange had barely begun when the House of Morgan began pouring orders in. On Monday alone, brokers bought 127,500 shares of Northern Pacific Common for the Morgan account. The price climbed from 114 to 127-1/2. On Tuesday the price hit 149. On Thursday it rose to 1,000.

A sudden, if brief, panic followed the boom, and many stocks went tumbling. But Hill-Morgan reached an understanding with Harriman. In what was really only a partial and temporary armistice, it was agreed that Harriman should have representation on the Northern Pacific board. Control of the three railroads, however, remained with the Hill-Morgan group. Hill continued to run the Northern Pacific, the Great Northern, and the Burlington.

Hill's plan for the three lines became apparent at once. His agents in the Orient prevailed on Japanese industrialists to try a shipment of American cotton to mix with the short-staple cotton from India that they were using. It proved successful, and from then on, the Hill lines carried an increasing tonnage of American cotton for shipment at Seattle. Minnesota flour began crossing the Pacific in huge volume. Hill carried the flour dirt-cheap to Seattle. In fact, his over-all policy was not to charge rates as high as the traffic could stand, but as low as the Hill lines could stand.

Four years after the armistice of 1901, the Hill-Harriman wars broke out anew. Harriman, through his Union Pacific and his large interest in the Northern Pacific, considered Oregon his domain. Hill thought differently. Before Harriman knew of it, Hill had completed surveys down the north bank of the Columbia River for a water-level route through the Cascade Mountains, which the Northern Pacific had originally planned to use but which it had deflected to the south bank.

No sooner had Hill's gangs started laying track down the north bank than they were met with legal harassments conjured up by Harriman. Then violence broke out in the field. Some of Hill's equipment was dynamited in night raids. Harriman's surveyors were shot at and driven off.

Hill won the north-bank fight, and his new line, the Portland & Seattle, was operated

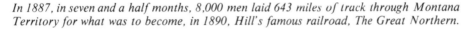

In 1887, in seven and a half months, 8,000 men laid 643 miles of track through Montana Territory for what was to become, in 1890, Hill's famous railroad, The Great Northern.

jointly by the Great Northern and the Northern Pacific. Yet he still was not content.

Posing as a wealthy sportsman, John F. Stevens, Hill's incomparable chief engineer, went into central Oregon to buy options on property along the Deschutes River. He also bought the charter for a nonexistent railroad, the Oregon Trunk, which had never laid a rail. Only then did Jim Hill announce that he planned to "open up" central Oregon by building 165 miles of railroad up the river to a place named Bend.

The news of Hill's plan to develop a region given over largely to sagebrush and lava beds gave Harriman a start. Almost nobody lived in the region. Harriman rightly foresaw that Hill planned to build right on through to San Francisco, and California was a Harriman province.

To parallel Hill's Oregon Trunk, Harriman hastily moved surveyors and laborers into the neighborhood, and they began laying track up the east bank of the Deschutes River. The Far West watched while the armies of the two railroad generals massed for an old-fashioned construction war.

In the narrow Deschutes Canyon, the opposing crews used dynamite on each other. For close fighting, the weapons were shovels, crowbars, and pick handles. The factions harassed each other's right of way with fences, barricades, and court orders. Armed guards occasionally lay flat on the rimrock to shoot at any mysterious movements below.

The campaign came to a head at the ranch of a man named Smith, who sold his property to Harriman. There was no other route to Bend except through this ranch. Hill decided to arbitrate. Harriman was willing. A truce was signed by which Hill agreed to build no farther south than Bend. But west of the Cascade Range the war continued, no longer with violence but with electric lines and steamships.

This struggle went on after Harriman died in 1909. It was not finished in 1916, when Hill died. Only by the mid-1920s, when the Great Northern at last gained entry to San Francisco, over the tracks of the Western Pacific, could the Hill-Harriman wars be said to be over. By then it was something of a hollow victory; in the very year that Harriman died, Henry Ford announced his Model T. One era was ending, a new one dawning.

But the legend of Jim Hill remains. He had walked on snowshoes across Minnesota in the days when the Sioux were on the warpath. By foot, horse, or rail he had been to all the limits reached by the Hill lines. When the Great Northern's foremost train, the *Empire Builder,* whistled for Sauk Centre or Whitefish or Spokane on its way 2,000 miles across the United States, the echoes found few buttes or valleys that Jim Hill had not seen himself.

Riding the Hill lines, one is likely to find certain qualities of Jim Hill the man. By this I mean the land, the climate, and the very towns and flag stops of this now spectacular, now monotonous, but often handsome, harsh, desolate, wild, and bitter region. Take little Malta, Montana, an angry sun beating, roasting the soil . . . or Havre, Montana, at night, snapping from cold, coyotes yelping within sound of the roundhouse . . . or Butte at twilight—Butte twinkling with astonishing brilliance in the thin air, seen from the Northern Pacific's limited as she comes suddenly out of the high pass of the Rockies, while away to the south stands the enormous stack marking Anaconda, spewing yellow flames and death to vegetation. . . . The Kootenai, a tumult of white water boiling over rocks, sea-green in the pools . . . then the immense lushness of the Wenatchee orchards . . . and at last the long, thundering bore straight through the Cascade Range and emergence into the silence of the towering firs, the most somber and melancholy forest on earth; then the lights of Puget Sound and the calls of ships bound for the Orient.

Jim Hill hitched these places together and tied them to Chicago, to Omaha, St. Louis, Kansas City, and Denver. They comprised the Hill lines. The Hill lines comprised an empire. Few other Americans had quite so much direct influence on quite so large a region.

Stewart H. Holbrook, an authority on American railroading, was author of James J. Hill *for the Knopf series, Great Lives in Brief.*

Volume 9

ENCYCLOPEDIC SECTION

The two-page reference guide below lists the entries by categories. The entries in this section supplement the subject matter covered in the text of this volume. A **cross-reference** (*see*) means that a separate entry appears elsewhere in this section. However, certain important persons and events mentioned here have individual entries in the Encyclopedic Section of another volume. Consult the Index in Volume 18.

BUSINESS AND INVENTION

Henry Comstock
Comstock Lode
Richard J. Gatling
Gatling gun
James J. Hill
Richard King

Norman Kittson
Joseph G. McCoy
William J. Palmer
Panic of 1857
Allan Pinkerton
placer mines
Jacob Schiff

DISASTERS

Blizzard of 1888
Chicago fire
Jeannette disaster

Johnstown flood
Peshtigo fire
Sultana disaster

FOREIGN RELATIONS

Alabama claims
Purchase of Alaska

Seward's Folly
Treaty of Washington

INDIANS

Black Kettle
Bozeman Trail
Bureau of Indian Affairs
Captain Jack
Cochise
Crazy Horse
Cut Nose
Dawes Severalty Act
Dull Knife
Geronimo

Ghost Dance Cult
Joseph
Kintpuash
Little Crow
Little Wolf
Mangas Coloradas
Red Cloud
Satank
Satanta
Sitting Bull

INDIAN WARS

buffalo soldiers
Henry B. Carrington
J. M. Chivington
Patrick Edward Connor
George A. Custer
Custer's Last Stand
William J. Fetterman

Battle of the Little Big Horn
Ranald S. Mackenzie
Nelson A. Miles
Marcus Reno
Joseph J. Reynolds
Sand Creek Massacre
Henry H. Sibley
Wounded Knee Massacre

REFORM MOVEMENTS AND LEADERS

Susan B. Anthony
Clara Barton
John Marshall Harlan
Helen Hunt Jackson

Molly Maguires
John Muir
Elizabeth Cady Stanton
woman suffrage

RELIGIOUS MOVEMENTS AND LEADERS

Christian Science
Mary Baker Eddy

Jehovah's Witnesses
Mennonites
Charles T. Russell

THOUGHT AND CULTURE

Lizzie Borden
Ned Buntline
Helen Hunt Jackson
Edward Z. C. Judson

John Muir
Pledge of Allegiance
Frederic Remington
Henry H. Richardson
Frederick Jackson Turner

WESTERN HEROES AND HOAXES

Billy the Kid
Calamity Jane
Great Diamond Fraud
Wild Bill Hickok

Isaac Parker
Peralta land fraud
Bill Pickett
Pikes Peak Hoax
Belle Starr

WESTWARD EXPANSION

Bozeman Trail
Camel Corps
Chisholm Trail
Henry Comstock
Comstock Lode
Desert Land Act
James J. Hill
Homestead Act

Norman Kittson
John Mullan
Oklahoma land rush
William J. Palmer
Pony Express
prairie schooner
Timber Culture Act
Wells Fargo

A

ALABAMA CLAIMS. This settlement of American claims against Great Britain for damages stemming from the Civil War was hailed as an important precedent in the peaceful settlement of international disputes. The United States had contended that the building of the *Alabama,* the *Florida,* the *Shenandoah,* and 10 other Confederate cruisers on British soil was a violation of Britain's obligations, under international law, as a neutral nation. In 1869, by a vote of 54 to 1, the Senate rejected the first official proposal to settle the dispute because it failed to include an apology from Britain or direct mention of the *Alabama* claims. Senator Charles Sumner (1811–1874) of Massachusetts then charged that not only did Britain owe $15,000,000 in direct damages, but that she also ought to pay more than $2,000,-000,000 in indirect damages for prolonging the war. He hinted that the cession of Canada would compensate the United States for the damages. However, a conciliatory attitude was taken by Hamilton Fish (1808–1893), who became Secretary of State in 1869. Two years earlier, Canada had become the first self-governing dominion in the British Commonwealth, thereby fulfilling its citizens' demands for independence. In addition, Britain in 1870 was having diplomatic difficulties with Russia, and she became worried that other nations, just as she had done, would build ships for the Russian fleet. Accordingly, Britain agreed to the **Treaty of Washington** (*see*) in 1871. This treaty included an apology from Britain and provided for an international tribunal to arbitrate both the direct and indirect damage claims. The American min-

ister to Britain, Charles Francis Adams (1807–1886), and representatives from Britain, Italy, Switzerland, and Brazil met in Geneva, Switzerland. In September, 1872, the arbitrators awarded $15,500,000 to the United States for the direct damages inflicted by the *Alabama,* the *Florida,* and the *Shenandoah,* rejected indirect damages, and absolved Britain of responsibility for the other ships.

ALASKA, Purchase of. In 1867, American Secretary of State William H. Seward (1801–1872) negotiated the purchase of Alaska from Russia for $7,200,000. The previous December, Russia had instructed its minister to the United States, Baron Edouard de Stoeckl, to attempt to sell Alaska. The Russian settlements there had proved unprofitable and also difficult to defend against the British in Canada. In the spring of 1867, Seward, who was an ardent expansionist, agreed to the purchase. He hoped not only to eliminate European possessions in the Americas, but also to link up Alaska with the United States by eventually annexing Canada (*see*

Alabama **claims**). A treaty was signed on March 30, 1867. Although reluctant to approve the purchase, the Senate ratified the treaty on April 9, chiefly out of gratitude to Russia for her support during the Civil War. The actual transfer of territory took place at Sitka, Alaska, on October 18, 1867. Many Americans were ignorant of Alaska's wealth in furs, timber, and metals and referred to the region as Seward's Folly and Seward's Icebox. The purchase added about 586,000 square miles of territory—more than twice the size of Texas—to the United States. The area was left as an unorganized territory and was so neglected that the Alaskans had to ask the British for help against the Indians in 1879. A governor was appointed in 1884, but Alaska was not organized as a territory until 1912, long after a gold strike in 1896 had brought about 30,000 people north. Alaska was admitted to the Union as the 49th state in 1959.

ANTHONY, Susan B. (1820–1906). Raised in a Quaker family, Miss Anthony became a dedicated

Demanding the right to vote, suffragettes march on the New York capital at Albany.

reformer, best known for her work in trying to obtain for women the right to vote. Her interest in reform began with the temperance movement. In 1852, when the Sons of Temperance refused to let her join because she was a female, Miss Anthony founded the Woman's State Temperance Society of New York. Miss Anthony was also an uncompromising abolitionist. Neither she nor her close associate, Elizabeth Cady Stanton (1815–1902), would support President Abraham Lincoln (1809–1865) until he issued the Emancipation Proclamation in 1863. After the Civil War, Miss Anthony demanded that the civil rights provisions of the Fourteenth and Fifteenth Amendments apply to women as well as to blacks. To publicize these efforts, she began publication of a weekly newspaper, *The Revolution*. Its motto was, "The true republic—men, their rights and nothing more; women, their rights and nothing less." In 1869, she and Mrs. Stanton formed the first national association to advocate women's suffrage. This group, the National Woman Suffrage Association, later merged with a similar organization and became the National American Woman Suffrage Association. Miss Anthony served as its president from 1892 to 1900. In 1872, Miss Anthony dared to vote in the Congressional election in Rochester, New York. She was arrested, tried, and fined, but refused to pay the fine and continued public-speaking tours. Near the close of the 19th century, she helped compile and edit four volumes of the six-volume *The History of Woman Suffrage*. At the age of 84, Miss Anthony went to Germany to help organize the International Woman Suffrage Alliance. She died 14 years before adoption of the amendment that gave women the vote.

B

BARTON, Clara (1821–1912). The founder of the American Red Cross, Miss Barton began her humanitarian career as a nurse during the Civil War. Throughout that conflict she procured badly needed supplies such as blankets and medicine and personally transported them to the battlefields, where she administered to the sick and wounded. This courageous service won her the nickname Angel of the Battlefields. After the war, she conducted a search for missing prisoners, and her records were used to identify the thousands of soldiers who died in the Confederate prison at Andersonville. In the course of a subsequent trip to Switzerland, undertaken because of poor health, Miss Barton joined the International Red Cross in Geneva and worked as a nurse behind German lines during the Franco-Prussian War of 1870. Because of its isolationist policies, the United States had refrained from joining the International Red Cross when it was founded in 1864. Miss Barton returned to America in 1873 determined to get her nation to join that organization. She was responsible for founding, almost single-handedly, the first chapter of the American

Clara Barton

Red Cross in 1881, and she promoted the Senate's ratification of the International Red Cross treaty the following year. In 1884, while attending an international conference in Geneva, Miss Barton secured passage of an amendment to the international treaty stipulating that during peacetime the Red Cross would aid victims of disasters such as floods, fires, and famines. She served as president of the American Red Cross from its beginning until 1904.

BILLY THE KID (1859?–1881). A legendary desperado of the American Southwest, Billy the Kid—who was born Henry McCarty—is believed to have committed more than 20 murders. He was gunned down by Pat Garrett (?–1908), his former gambling partner, who was chosen as a sheriff of Lincoln County in the New Mexico Territory expressly to capture Billy. The Kid was probably born in New York City. About 1862, he moved with his parents to Kansas, where his father apparently died. Billy's mother remarried in Santa Fe in March, 1873, and settled in the New Mexico Territory. Billy was soon hanging around saloons and gambling houses. It is said that at the age of 12 he stabbed a man to death for insulting his mother, but there is no evidence of this. His first verified murder—that of a blacksmith—occurred in 1877, three years after the death of his mother. Billy subsequently changed his name to William H. Bonney. Following other violent adventures, he was hired as a gunman in cattle wars in the Pecos Valley in 1878. He then engaged in large-scale cattle rustling. After taking part in the slaying of a sheriff and his deputy in April, 1878, Billy was captured two years later by Garrett and a posse at Stinking Springs, in the New Mexico Ter-

Dime novels glamorized the life of the notorious killer William Bonney.

ritory, and sentenced to die. Despite shackles and handcuffs, he killed two guards and escaped. Garrett pursued him to Fort Sumner and shot and killed him on July 14, 1881. The legend created in contemporary dime novels and biographies stressed the non-chalance and cheerfulness with which the left-handed Billy dispatched his victims.

BLACK KETTLE (?–1868). Black Kettle was an important chief of the Southern Cheyennes who were living in eastern Colorado in the early 1860s. Fearing that his people would be wiped out if they continued to resist the white man, Black Kettle reported his intention to live in peace to military officials at nearby Fort Lyon. He then established a village of about 700 Southern Cheyennes and Arapahos on Sand Creek, about 30 miles from the fort. On November 27, 1864, in one of the most notorious episodes of the Indian wars, about 750 cavalry volunteers led by Colonel **J. M. Chivington** (*see*) suddenly descended on the quiet village and slaughtered about 160 of the Indians. Black Kettle's wife was killed in the **Sand**

Creek Massacre (*see*), but the chief escaped. Most of the surviving Cheyennes fled north, where they warned other tribes of the white man's treachery and went on the warpath. Black Kettle, however, continued to seek peace. With a small band of followers, he migrated southward. In the fall of 1868, he camped on the Washita River in Indian Territory (Oklahoma). Again he made peace overtures, this time to nearby Fort Cobb. However, on November 29, 1868, about 800 troops of the Seventh Cavalry under Lieutenant Colonel **George A. Custer** (*see*) surprised and destroyed the Indian encampment. Black Kettle, with about 40 of his people, was killed

BLIZZARD OF 1888. The worst blizzard recorded in American history began as a snowstorm on Sunday, March 11, 1888. For three days, a heavy snow fell, burying cities and villages in the northeastern United States and bringing normal activity to a standstill. Chill winds piled up drifts as high as 30 feet on some New York City streets. According to the New York Weather Bureau, which has been collecting data since 1869, 21 inches of snow fell in Central Park between midnight on March 12 and three o'clock in the afternoon on March 14. Freezing temperatures turned the waters of the East River to ice. Transportation drew to a halt, and people not snowbound in their homes were reduced to traveling by foot or sleigh. Fire trucks were unable to move through the clogged streets, and fires were left to burn themselves out. All railroads ceased operation, telegraph lines fell, and businesses and the New York Stock Exchange closed. By the time the Great Blizzard was over, it had caused 400 deaths and a property loss estimated at $25,000,000.

BORDEN, Lizzie Andrew (1860–1927). Lizzie Borden was accused of the ax murders of her father and stepmother in their Fall River, Massachusetts, home on August 4, 1892. She was acquitted in June, 1893, following a sensational trial, but remained an object of suspicion throughout her life. Her supposed guilt is commemorated in a popular children's jingle, *"Lizzie Borden took an ax / And gave her mother forty whacks. / When she saw what she had done, / She gave her father forty-one."* Lizzie's mother died when the girl was only two years old. Her father, a wealthy mill owner, remarried three years later. Lizzie and her two sisters disliked the stepmother, calling her Mrs. Borden. As a young woman, Lizzie's activities included teaching Sunday school, and membership in the Christian Endeavor Society, the

Lizzie Borden

Fruit and Flower Mission Society, and the Woman's Christian Temperance Union. On August 2, 1892, Mr. and Mrs. Borden became violently ill. They suspected poisoning. Two days later, their mutilated bodies were discovered in their home. A great deal of circumstantial evidence pointed to Lizzie—she was caught in several lies surrounding the deaths and was found burning a dress in a stove—but she was acquitted. Shunned by her neighbors, Lizzie continued to live in Fall River until her death in 1927. She has been immortalized in music, literature, and legend.

BOZEMAN TRAIL. The Bozeman Trail was the shortest route from Julesburg, in present-day Colorado, to the goldfields near Virginia City, in what is now Montana. The trail, which ran about 500 miles through the hunting grounds of the Sioux Indians, was marked out by John Bozeman (1835–1867), a Georgia miner. Bozeman set out in 1863 to find a road that would connect the goldfields directly with the Oregon Trail and eliminate roundabout routes via Fort Hall, Idaho, and Fort Benton on the Missouri River. He found a pass, later named after him, between Virginia City and the Yellowstone River Valley. After crossing this pass, the Bozeman Trail ran east around the north end of the Big Horn Mountains, then turned southeast until it joined the North Platte River and the Oregon Trail, 70 miles west of Fort Laramie. The route was a smooth, grassy one, suitable for wagon trains hauling supplies to the goldfields. Hundreds of wagons soon chose the Bozeman Trail over the longer, rougher routes. However, the Sioux resented the trespassing and attacked travelers using the route. To protect the caravans, the federal government constructed three forts along the Bozeman Trail during 1865 and 1866. The first, Fort Connor (later Fort Reno), was established where the trail crossed the principal branch of the Powder River. The second, Fort Philip Kearny, was constructed 65 miles farther north, and the third post, Fort C. P.

Smith, was built where the route crossed the Big Horn River in Montana. Indian attacks continued until the signing of the second Fort Laramie Treaty in 1868, when the government abandoned the posts. The year before, Bozeman himself had been killed on the trail. The trail was reopened in 1877, after the Sioux had been suppressed. It became a popular route for driving cattle north from Texas to Montana and Wyoming. Interstate 90 now parallels the trail at many points.

BUFFALO SOLDIERS. The black troopers of the Ninth and the Tenth Cavalry Regiments—called buffalo soldiers by the Indians— played a central role in pacifying the American West. After the Civil War, many black soldiers— especially those who had been slaves but now had no homes— wished to remain in uniform. In 1866, Ulysses S. Grant (1822– 1885), then commander in chief of the army, ordered the formation of two all-black cavalry regiments—the Ninth, under Colonel Edward Hatch (1832–1889), and the Tenth, commanded by Colonel Benjamin H. Grierson (1826– 1911). Congress, in authorizing the black units, had insisted that all officers be white, and there was difficulty in obtaining qualified and willing leaders. In addition, the black soldiers were often provided with shoddy equipment and supplied with poor horses. Nevertheless, by 1867 both regiments were on duty on the frontier. The Ninth Cavalry was sent to the badlands of western Texas, where it fought the Mescalero and Lipan Apaches and the Kickapoos. Transferred to the District of New Mexico in 1875, the cavalrymen battled Chiricahua Apaches, hostile Mexicans, and white bandits. They were dispatched to the Indian Territory (Oklahoma) in

1881 to prevent white settlers from stealing Indian land. After a largely uneventful tour in the Wyoming Territory (1885–1890), the Ninth helped put down the Sioux uprising in the Dakotas brought on by the **Ghost Dance Cult** (*see*) in 1890. Most of the Tenth Cavalry went initially to Kansas, where they guarded the builders of the Kansas Pacific Railroad and cleared the state of Cheyenne Indians. In 1869, the headquarters of the Tenth was moved to Camp Wichita (later Fort Sill), in Indian Territory, where the unit's 12 companies supervised the settlement of Indians on reservations and skirmished with renegade Comanches and Kiowas under **Satanta** and **Satank** (*see both*). In 1873, most of the Tenth joined the Ninth in the Indian wars in Texas. The final major campaign of the Tenth against the Indian came in 1885– 1886, when the battle-hardened regiment went to Arizona to assist in the defeat of Apaches under **Mangas Coloradas** and **Geronimo** (*see both*). John J. Pershing (1860– 1948), who would lead the American Expeditionary Force in World War I, led the Tenth Cavalry's Troop H as a lieutenant in rounding up several unruly bands of Cree Indians in 1896—an assignment that later earned Pershing the nickname Black Jack. Both regiments also explored and mapped remote areas of the Southwest, strung telegraph lines, guarded wagon trains, and built forts. Thirteen black soldiers of the two regiments won the Medal of Honor. Both units later served with distinction in the Spanish-American War in 1898.

BUNTLINE, Ned (1823–1886). Edward Zane Carroll Judson— known by his pen name, Ned Buntline—is credited with originating the dime novel. Born in

New York State, Buntline ran away to sea when he was only 11. He was at different times a midshipman, a soldier, a fur trader, a magazine editor, an organizer of the Know-Nothing Party, an actor, and a playwright. Buntline also shot a man, was lynched but cut down alive by a friend, spent time in prison for bigamy and instigating a riot, and gave temperance lectures while drunk. He called himself Colonel, though he had never held a rank above sergeant and was dismissed from the Union Army in 1864 for drunkenness. His literary career had begun shortly after he resigned from the navy in 1842. Buntline founded a magazine, *Ned Buntline's Own,* which contained sensational stories. He was a prolific writer, once taking only 62 hours to compose a 600-page novel. In all, Buntline wrote more than 400 books, all of them cheap, paper-covered publications that sold for 10¢. They included such titles as *Magdalena, The Beautiful Mexican Maid* (1847), *Norwood, or Life on the Prairie* (1849), and *Stella Delorme, or, the Comanche's Dream* (1860). Buntline and other dime novelists depicted the romance and adventure of the West and often created heroes for the public. In 1869, Buntline met the then unknown William F. Cody (1846–1917) and dubbed him Buffalo Bill in a story called "Buffalo Bill, the King of the Border Men." Cody was an overnight sensation and next appeared in Buntline's play, *The Scouts of the Plains,* a critical failure but a huge financial success. Buntline continued to write dime novels until his death.

BUREAU OF INDIAN AFFAIRS.
For nearly 150 years, government relations with the various tribes throughout the nation have been handled by the Bureau of Indian Affairs. The War Department had been responsible for the job since 1789, but westward expansion created the necessity for a separate bureau. The bureau, which was set up within the War Department in 1824, was to control trade with the Indians, protect them from exploitation, and supervise their concentration on reservations. Indian sympathizers criticized the bureau's harsh treatment of the Indians, and this, together with requests from Westerners, led in 1849 to the transfer of the bureau to the newly organized Department of the Interior. However, the transfer failed to improve the bureau's record. "Indian rings" of crooked agents and suppliers swindled many tribes, and Indian families on reservations suffered. Indian agents, whose authority stemmed from the Indian Intercourse Act of 1834, were appointed largely on the basis of political connections and were often guilty of corruption, indifference, or stupidity. The army wanted the bureau to be turned back to the War Department. It claimed that the bureau mismanaged affairs until things got out of hand and then called on the army for help. On the other hand, some bureau officials objected to the army's brutal treatment of the Indians. One major reform attempt had been made in 1869 when a Seneca Indian, Ely S. Parker (1828–1895), an engineer who had been a Union brigadier general in the Civil War, was appointed commissioner. However, he resigned two years later after unfounded charges of fraud were brought against him. The bureau became little more than a land-administering agency, especially after the **Dawes Severalty Act** (*see*) of 1887 broke up tribal landholdings. The bureau continues to exist today, protecting the interests of about 787,000 Indians on approximately 53,000,000 acres and promoting vocational programs.

C

CALAMITY JANE (1852?–1903).
Hard-drinking and sharpshooting Martha Jane Burke—popularly known as Calamity Jane—was one of the wildest women in the West. Born in either Missouri or Illinois about 1852, she moved on to Wyoming, where, when she was about 17, her playmates were the rough railroad gangs around the city of Cheyenne. In 1875, when she was about 23, Calamity dressed herself as a man and joined a geological expedition into

Calamity Jane

the Black Hills of present-day South Dakota. The next year, her appetite for adventure still unsatisfied, she again masqueraded as a man to accompany an expedition led by General George Crook (1829–1890) against the Sioux and Northern Cheyennes. Calamity Jane marched out of Fort Fetterman with his supply train, the only woman among 1,300 men. Calamity's thirst for alcohol equaled her other appetites and reduced her to unfortunate circumstances. To support herself in later years, she appeared in dime museums and peddled inexpensive copies of her memoirs. She was reportedly married to a number of men, including **Wild Bill Hickok** (*see*), but no proof of any marriage exists.

CAMEL CORPS. In 1855, Secretary of War Jefferson Davis (1808–1889) persuaded Congress to appropriate $30,000 for the purchase of camels to be used as pack animals during the army's exploration of the Southwest. Davis believed that the camels, which can go for long periods without water, would make it easier for explorers in the arid Southwest. Two officers were sent to the camel markets in Alexandria, Egypt, and Smyrna, Turkey, where they paid $250 apiece for the first 33 dromedaries. In all they purchased 76. The animals were shipped back to Camp Verde, Texas, where the First Camel Corps was organized. To educate soldiers accustomed to mules and horses on how to handle the camels, six Arabs were hired to return with them. Twenty-eight of the animals were sent to California in 1857 for use on mail routes through the deserts. The other camels were first used that same year to survey a road from Fort Defiance, in New Mexico Territory, to the eastern border of Cal-

ifornia. The animals' ability to carry more and travel faster than mules contributed to the success of the assignment and seemed to justify the existence of the camel corps. However, horses and mules bolted in fright at the sight of the camels, and army mule skinners (drivers) came to detest them. When prodded to rise with excessive loads, the camels would often spit in the soldiers' faces. Some even attacked and killed drivers. The corps was abandoned in 1863, when the remaining camels were auctioned off, some to circuses, others to mining companies to haul freight to mines in Nevada. When the use of camels was outlawed in that state because of their ferocity, the animals were driven back to the Arizona Territory and turned loose. Occasionally cowboys or prospectors would encounter a stray camel in the desert and, more often than not, use it for target practice. One was found in 1873, wandering in the Arizona Territory, with a corpse lashed to its hump. Years later, wild camels were still reported in the Southwest.

CAPTAIN JACK (1837?–1873). In the early 1870s, the federal government was determined to place the Indians of the Northwest on reservations. Captain Jack, a leader of the Modocs, who lived along the border between Oregon and California, was equally determined to resist confinement. His real name was Kintpuash, or Kientpoos, but white men had dubbed him Captain Jack because of his love of ribbons, medals, and military glitter. On November 29, 1872, Jack rose up against the soldiers who had come to "resettle" his people and fled, with 250 followers, to the lava caves south of Tule Lake in California (*see p. 797*). For four months, Jack's band—no more than 80

of whom were warriors—held off more than 400 soldiers. His position in the lava beds was virtually impregnable. Army casualties mounted, and a peace conference was called for April 11, 1873. However, during the negotiations, Jack shot and killed General E. R. S. Canby (1817–1873) and a clergyman. He then resumed the fighting, wearing the slain general's uniform. Enraged, President Ulysses S. Grant (1822–1885) called for action from his army chief, William T. Sherman (1820–1891), who responded, "You will be fully justified in their utter extermination." More than 1,000 troops, enemy Indians, and amateur Indian fighters converged on the lava beds. The Modocs were finally shelled from their rock fortress by artillery in June, 1873. On October 3, that same year, at Fort Klamath, Oregon, Captain Jack and his chief lieutenants—Sconchin John, Black Jim, and Boston Charley—were hanged.

CARRINGTON, Henry Beebee (1824–1912). An army colonel, Carrington was in charge of building forts along the **Bozeman Trail** (*see*) in the present-day states of Wyoming and Montana. It was Carrington who, as commander of Fort Philip Kearny, in what is now Nebraska, was blamed for the ill-fated mission in which Captain **William J. Fetterman** (*see*) and his detachment of 80 men were slain. For two years, Carrington fought continually against the Sioux Indians under **Red Cloud** (*see*) before the federal government decided to abandon the Bozeman Trail in 1868. A native of Wallingford, Connecticut, and a graduate (1845) of Yale, Carrington had combined several successful careers before going West to fight Indians. Between 1845 and 1848, as a teacher at Irving Institute at Tarrytown,

New York, and at New Haven Collegiate Institute, in Connecticut, he began a writing career, which over the years resulted in many publications, including books on military history and Indian affairs. Carrington practiced law for 12 years (1848–1860) in Columbus, Ohio, where he was a prominent abolitionist and Republican. When the Civil War broke out, Carrington, who was adjutant general of the Ohio militia, helped to keep what became the state of West Virginia in the Union by dispatching nine regiments across the Ohio River. During the war, he recruited and trained thousands of troops for the Union Army. After Carrington's two-year war with Red Cloud, he was assigned to protect the Union Pacific Railroad from Indian attacks. He later became a professor of military science (1869–1878) at Wabash College in Indiana. Carrington was responsible for negotiating a treaty with the Flathead Indians of Montana in 1889.

CHICAGO FIRE. According to legend, on the evening of Sunday, October 8, 1871, a cow owned by Mrs. Patrick O'Leary of Chicago kicked over a kerosine lantern and started a fire that spread throughout that city, burning down most of it. Although Mrs. O'Leary later said that she had not carried a lantern to her milking shed that night, the great fire did originate somewhere near her home on De-Koven Street, on the city's West Side. A stiff wind blew the flames north and east until three and a half square miles of Chicago, a city built of wood, were reduced to ashes. Between nine o'clock Sunday night and 10:30 Monday night, 250 lives were lost, 17,450 buildings were destroyed, and nearly 100,000 people were left homeless. An estimated total of

$200,000,000 in damages was incurred. At midnight Sunday, the sky over central Chicago was filled with burning coals, which were sucked up by the wind from the main fire and dropped elsewhere to start others. Describing the night, a fireman said, "You couldn't see anything over you but fire . . . . No clouds, no stars, nothing else but fire." Thousands of people fled before the flames, pushing belongings in front of them in buggies, wheelbarrows, baby carriages—anything with wheels. Convicts were released from the endangered city prison. Expecting the fires to destroy their stock, saloonkeepers gave away bottles of whiskey, and jewelers passed out gems. Late Monday, a steady rain began to fall, and by Tuesday all the fires were nearly extinguished. Martial law was temporarily imposed on the city, and supplies of food and clothing started to pour in. Relief came in such amounts that Chicago's nine railroads were unable to transport it all. Nearly $5,000,-000,000 in contributions from all

over the world was donated, and the city began to rebuild itself. The Chicago *Tribune* predicted that the city "shall rise again!" Within two years, the burned-out area had been rebuilt and was worth more than the destruction caused by the fire. The wide publicity that the Chicago fire received in the nation's newspapers obscured the more tragic **Peshtigo fire** (*see*) that occurred on the same night. Nearly 1,200 lives were lost when that Wisconsin town and nearby areas were completely destroyed.

CHISHOLM TRAIL. After the Civil War, hundreds of thousands of cattle were driven north from Texas to Abilene, Kansas, over the Chisholm Trail, a distance of more than 650 miles. Although some cattle had previously been shipped north from Texas, the postwar years brought a huge increase in the demand for beef in the Northeast. Cattle selling for $4 a head in Texas brought $40 a head in Chicago. In 1866, about 250,000 head were driven north

As flames light the night, Chicagoans flee across the Randolph Street Bridge.

to Sedalia, Missouri, the nearest rail connection to the Northeast. However, this route led both through settled areas, where local farmers objected, and through wooded areas, where it was hard to control the cattle. In 1867, **Joseph G. McCoy** (*see*) purchased the town of Abilene. He had surveyors map a trail across the open plains from Texas and arranged for railroad transportation north. McCoy shipped 35,000 cattle from Abilene that first year. By 1869, 150,000 cattle had been shipped north from Abilene. The trail from San Antonio, Texas, to Abilene was named after Jesse Chisholm (1806–1868), a half-breed Indian trader. His wagon tracks had been the first to mark part of the trail route, from Wichita, Kansas, to the Washita River Valley in Indian Territory (Oklahoma) in the mid-1860s. The Chisholm Trail began to decline in importance with the extension of the railroad west to Ellsworth and Dodge City, Kansas, in the 1870s.

CHIVINGTON, John Milton (1821–1894). As a colonel of the Colorado Volunteers, Chivington led his troops into battle against a group of unsuspecting Cheyenne Indians with the order, "Kill and scalp all, big and little; nits make lice." The result was the **Sand Creek Massacre** (*see*), where about 160 Indians, the majority of them women and children, were slain. Born in Ohio, Chivington became a Methodist minister in 1844, and, four years later, moved west to spread the Gospel among the Indians as well as the white man. Chivington became known as the Fighting Parson when he fought in the Kansas border wars against advocates of slavery. In 1861, he was appointed a major in the Colorado Volunteers and was later promoted to colonel. He

gained a reputation as a sound military leader in campaigns against the Confederates in the New Mexico Territory. In 1863, he was appointed commander of the military district of Colorado. Anxious to make war against the Indians to further his own political ambitions, Chivington ordered about 750 soldiers under his command out against **Black Kettle** (*see*) and an estimated 700 Cheyennes, who had already accepted peace terms. On November 29, 1864, the Indians were encamped at Sand Creek, near Fort Lyon, Colorado. Ignoring Black Kettle's white flag, Chivington ordered his men to attack. He and his men were later received as heroes in Denver, even appearing in a theater at intermission to display scalps. The rest of the nation, however, was not so pleased, and Chivington resigned his commission to avoid a court-martial. In 1868, a Congressional investigating committee reported that the Sand Creek Massacre ". . . scarcely has its parallel in the records of Indian barbarity." Although he later held local governmental offices, Chivington's hopes of a national political career were ended.

CHRISTIAN SCIENCE. *See* **Eddy, Mary Baker.**

COCHISE (1815?–1874). A chief of the Chiricahua Apaches in Arizona, Cochise waged war against white soldiers and settlers from 1861 until 1872. In the Southwest, his fame as a warrior was matched only by that of another Chiricahua, **Geronimo** (*see*). The Chiricahua Apaches had been at peace with the Americans before 1861. In February of that year, Cochise and three other Apache tribal chieftains were taken prisoner while conferring with a headstrong young army lieutenant under a flag of truce. His Indian compan-

ions were hanged, but Cochise, despite three bullet wounds, escaped. For 10 years, he wreaked bloodcurdling revenge upon the white invader. He made peace in 1871, only to find himself and his people relocated to the New Mexico Territory the next year. Cochise escaped from the reservation with 200 followers, but he soon agreed to cease hostilities. He died in 1874 while living quietly on the Chiricahua Reservation in New Mexico. A county and a mountain in Arizona bear his name.

COMSTOCK, Henry. *See* **Comstock Lode.**

COMSTOCK LODE. The Comstock Lode was one of the richest silver and gold deposits ever discovered in America. The vein ran lengthwise along the Virginia Range in western Nevada. It and adjoining pockets of ore called bonanzas yielded between $300,-000,000 and $500,000,000 in silver and gold from the time of their discovery in 1859 to 1879, when the deposits had paid out. The lode was named for Henry Comstock (1820–1870), a shaggy California prospector who had purchased a share from the two miners who discovered the lode, Peter O'Riley and Pat McLaughlin. Comstock in turn sold his interest for $11,000, taking $10 as a down payment for claims later worth millions of dollars. When the news of the discovery reached California, a human stampede began across the Sierra Nevada to Carson Valley. Miners, speculators, traders, and gamblers, all hoping to make their fortune, walked and rode over the mountains to descend by the thousands on Virginia City, Nevada. With a population swollen to nearly 40,-000, the city was described as a collection of "Frame shanties, pitched together as if by accident: tents of canvas, of blankets, of brush, of potato-sacks and old shirts, with empty whiskey-barrels for chimneys. . . ." Although a few men, such as John W. Mackay (1831–1902) and George Hearst (1820–1891), the father of newspaper publisher William Randolph Hearst (1863–1951), became multimillionaires, the majority of miners never hit pay dirt. Of the 4,000 claims staked on the lode, only 300 were actually mined, and only 20 were considered worthwhile investments. Comstock himself futilely searched throughout present-day Montana and Idaho for "another Comstock," but, having failed, finally committed suicide. Virginia City is now a ghost town.

CONNOR, Patrick Edward (1820–1891). An Indian fighter, Connor headed the army's unsuccessful Powder River expedition, which set out from Fort Laramie in 1865 to suppress the Sioux, Cheyennes, and Arapahoes in what is now northeastern Wyoming. A soldier at 19, Connor took part in fighting the Seminoles from 1839 to 1842. As a member of the Texas Volunteers, he later took part in the Mexican War. At the outbreak of the Civil War, Connor was appointed colonel of the Third California Infantry. While in command of the Military District of Utah in 1863, he led 200 troops in wiping out most of a band of Bannock and Shoshone Indians that had harassed the Bear River region of present-day Idaho for 15 years. For this victory, which opened the area to peaceful settlement, Connor was promoted to brigadier general and later acclaimed as the Liberator of Utah. In 1865, he was given command of the District of the Plains and ordered to round up the Sioux, Cheyennes, and Arapahoes around the Powder River. With Jim

Bridger (1804–1881) guiding them, Connor and 900 men marched out of Fort Laramie on July 30, 1865. After pausing to establish Fort Connor (later Fort Reno), on the **Bozeman Trail** (*see*), Connor pushed on to the Tongue River, where he destroyed an Arapaho village on August 29. However, two other columns of the expedition, ill-supplied with maps, lost their way and broke ranks. The campaign was therefore considered a failure and the blame fell on Connor. Furious, he returned to Utah without bothering to file an official report. After his subsequent dismissal from the army in 1866, Connor settled in Utah, where he actively promoted the territory's mining interests, published its first non-Mormon newspaper, the *Union Vidette*, and operated the first steamboat on the Great Salt Lake.

CRAZY HORSE (1845?–1877). A famous Sioux chief who led his warriors into battle with the cry, "Come on, Dakotas, it's a good day to die," Crazy Horse headed the attack on General **George A. Custer** and his troops at **Custer's Last Stand** (*see both*) on the Little Big Horn River. It is said that he was named when a wild horse stampeded through the Indian camp at the time of his birth. Little is known of Crazy Horse until he became chief of the Oglala tribe of Sioux. In 1875, Crazy Horse and his tribe, which was near starvation, illegally left their agencies (restricted areas on the reservation) in the Black Hills of the Dakota Territory to hunt for food. They were also angry at the white prospectors who had been entering the Black Hills to search for gold. On June 17, 1876, Crazy Horse attacked General George Crook (1829–1890) on the Rosebud River in present-day Montana and forced him to retreat. He then moved north to the Little Big

Horn River to meet **Sitting Bull** (*see*) and other Sioux and Cheyenne chiefs. There, on June 25, he attacked Custer and his men. After the massacre, the army made every effort to capture Crazy Horse. In January, 1877, General **Nelson A. Miles** (*see*) broke up the Oglala winter camp near the Rosebud River. The tribe escaped, but spent most of the winter again without food. In May, Crazy Horse and his tribe of about 1,000 men, women, and children surrendered at the Red Cloud Agency near Camp Robinson, Nebraska. He was later arrested when Chief **Joseph** (*see*) of the Nez Perce stirred up trouble in the northern Plains. Authorities feared the two chiefs would join. A guard stabbed and killed Crazy Horse with a bayonet when he resisted being locked up.

CUSTER, George Armstrong (1839–1876). A dashing, controversial cavalry officer, Custer died with his entire command at a battle on the Little Big Horn River, in present-day Montana, that is known as **Custer's Last Stand** (*see*). Custer graduated last in his class at West Point in 1861 and fought in the First Battle of Bull Run that year. In 1863, when he was 23 years old, he was promoted to the rank of brigadier general, the youngest American ever to attain that position. After the Civil War, Custer was assigned to the Seventh Cavalry at Fort Riley, Kansas. Often insubordinate, he was court-martialed in 1867 for deserting his command to visit his wife during a cholera scare and was relieved of his command. General Philip Sheridan (1831–1888), who had been impressed with Custer during the Civil War, managed to have Custer restored to command in 1868. Custer spent the next few years building a wide reputation as an Indian fighter,

General Custer wards off a Sioux brave in Cassilly Adams' imaginative painting of Custer's Last Stand.

and in 1874 he published a book, *My Life on the Plains,* detailing his exploits. That same year, he led an exploring expedition into the Black Hills of the Dakota Territory. The discovery of gold in that area and the subsequent influx of settlers triggered the events that culminated at the Little Big Horn River. Early in 1876, Custer was included in army plans to round up hostile Sioux and Cheyennes in the Dakota Territory. However, at his own request, he went to Washington, D.C., to testify about a scandal in the administration of President Ulysses S. Grant (1822–1885). Custer's hearsay testimony implicating Grant's own brother, Orvil Grant (1835–1881), so angered the President that he removed Custer from command. Only public protests and a plea from General Alfred A. Terry (1827–1890) enabled Custer to undertake his fateful mission. Terry ordered Custer to help drive the Indians from the Black Hills, where gold had been found, and confine them to limited areas of their reservations. Custer's orders were to locate the Indians and, using Terry's personal scout, to relay the information to two other columns of troops. On his march, Custer did not follow the route

outlined by Terry and arrived near the Little Big Horn River on June 25, a day early. The Indians had already discovered his presence, and Custer decided to attack immediately instead of waiting for the other columns to appear. The Indians, estimated at between 2,000 and 4,000 strong, annihilated Custer and nearly 250 men in less than half an hour. To some, Custer was a peerless soldier and Indian fighter, who died bravely against overwhelming odds. His widow, Elizabeth Bacon Custer (1842–1933), devoted much of her life to perpetuating this memory and blaming Major **Marcus Reno** (*see*) for the defeat. To others, however, Custer was a braggart who willfully disobeyed orders and risked the lives of his men to seek glory for himself.

CUSTER'S LAST STAND. On June 25, 1876, near the Little Big Horn River in present-day Montana, five companies of the Seventh Cavalry led by **George A. Custer** (*see*) were annihilated by a combined force of Sioux and Cheyenne Indians. Earlier, in 1875, the Indians, who faced a harsh winter and were near starvation, left the agencies on their reservations in the Dakota Terri-

tory to hunt for food. The **Bureau of Indian Affairs** (*see*) ordered them to return to the agencies by January 31, 1876. Many Indians did not learn of the order and others found it impossible to break up their winter camps to obey the order. When the Indians did not comply, troops were ordered out against them. Custer was sent forward to the Little Big Horn River with about 650 men, including Indian scouts, civilian guides, and interpreters. The plan was for Custer to locate the enemy and join two other columns of troops for the attack. He arrived near the Indian encampment about noon on June 25. Between 2,000 and 4,000 warriors, many more than had been expected, were gathered there. Custer's presence had been detected by the Indians, and he decided to attack immediately rather than wait for the other two columns. He split his regiment into four battalions, with himself commanding the largest. Major **Marcus Reno** (*see*) and Captain Frederick Benteen (1834–1898) each commanded a battalion, and a pack train followed behind. Reno's force was attacked after it had crossed the river and was forced to retreat. Benteen's force joined Reno's, and they were engaged defending themselves until the following day. Meanwhile, Custer, with about 250 men, determined to attack the Indian village, which he apparently thought the Indians were abandoning. Some historians believe he was hoping to trap the Indians between his force and Reno's. However, the Indians attacked him. They were led by the Oglala Sioux chief **Crazy Horse** (*see*), who had combined forces with two Hunkpapa Sioux chiefs, **Sitting Bull** (*see*) and Gall (1840?–1894). The battle lasted less than half an hour, and the only survivor from Custer's side was a horse named Comanche. Because none of Custer's men survived, and the Indians did not tell their story until years later, controversies have developed over details of the battle. Reno and Benteen were accused of not supporting Custer because of their personal dislike of him. In 1879, a court of inquiry exonerated them of any guilt. Custer has been alternately viewed as a great hero and a reckless fool. The battle itself was of little military significance, except that the American public demanded an immediate end to the Indian menace. Many painters have tried to depict the battle scene (*see pp. 786–787*) of what has since been called Custer's Last Stand. For years afterward, Comanche—saddled but riderless—was led at cavalry parades to commemorate the men of Custer's command.

CUT NOSE (?–1862). A Santee Sioux who earned his name by biting off part of an enemy's nose, Cut Nose was one of the warriors who took part in the Minnesota Massacre of 1862 (*see pp. 778–779*). The Indian attacks, led by **Little Crow** (*see*), began on August 17 and continued for nearly

six weeks. Cut Nose killed white settlers "till his arm was tired." The first day of the uprising, he had his thumb nearly bitten off by a mortally wounded farmer whose house his war party had attacked. When Colonel **Henry Sibley** (*see*) and a force of 1,600 soldiers suppressed the Sioux in late September and October, Cut Nose was one of almost 2,000 Indians who were captured. He was tried with more than 400 other Indians for murder and looting and was one of 306 who were condemned to death. Although the majority of the sentences were commuted, Cut Nose and 37 other Santee Sioux were hanged on the day after Christmas, 1862, at Mankato, Minnesota. Doctors from nearby towns witnessed the hangings with more than idle interest. They had drawn lots among themselves for the bodies of the condemned men, hoping to use the skeletons in their medical practice. The body of Cut Nose was appropriated by Dr. William Mayo (1819–1911), who used the skeleton to teach anatomy. Later, Mayo founded the world-famous Mayo Clinic at Rochester, Minnesota.

D

DAWES SEVERALTY ACT. Passed in 1887, this act established Indian policy in the United States for nearly half a century. The act marked a new effort by the nation to "civilize" the Indians and turn them into individual homeowners. Many humanitarians such as **Helen Hunt Jackson** (*see*) supported it as a way of bringing the Indian into the mainstream of American life. The act provided that all the tribal landholdings be subdivided into individual homesteads of 160 acres each, which would then be distributed among tribal

members. To protect an Indian's property, he could not sell his land for 25 years. After that time, he was to be granted full citizenship. Although well-intentioned, the act did not have the desired effect. After the Indians received their land allotments, the surplus of the tribal holdings went to white settlers. The Indian lands were usually inferior to the surplus land. In addition, the Indians were not farmers by tradition and, on their poor land, had little incentive to become homesteaders. Thus many of them found it impossible to earn a living, and land speculators cheated them into leasing their lands at ridiculously low prices. Seven years before the act was passed, Indian tribes had controlled 150,000,000 acres of land. By the time the Indian Reorganization Act was passed in 1934, these Indians had lost possession of more than 90,000,000 acres of their old tribal landholdings to the white man.

DESERT LAND ACT. To encourage settlement of the arid West, Congress enacted the Desert Land Act in 1877, which provided that a settler could acquire 640 acres of land for $160. If within three years he irrigated the land, he could purchase the property outright upon payment of an additional $1 an acre. More than 2,600,000 acres of land were claimed under the act, but more than 95% of the claims were fraudulent. Because claim holders could transfer their rights, cattlemen eager to gain title to grazing land made their cowboys and hired hands file claims that were then signed over to the cattlemen. The ranchers sidestepped the irrigation requirement by having their cowhands testify that they "had seen water on the claim," often after a cup of water was poured on the ground.

DULL KNIFE (dates unknown). Also known as Morning Star, this Northern Cheyenne chief helped to lead his people in flight from the army in the late 1870s. Like **Little Wolf** (*see*), Dull Knife had agreed to leave his home in Montana, lured by government promises of a good life on the Cheyenne-Arapaho Reservation in Indian Territory (Oklahoma). In 1878, after a year and a half in a malaria-infested area where no buffalo roamed and the **Bureau of Indian Affairs** (*see*) failed to supply enough food, Dull Knife resolved to leave. Struggling northward with Little Wolf and a band of almost 300 Cheyenne, they managed to fight off government troops until Dull Knife and his group separated from Little Wolf halfway through Nebraska. While heading northwest in driving snow in the direction of Wyoming, Dull Knife's party of about 180 Cheyennes was met unexpectedly by cavalry troops from Camp Robinson. Without fighting, Dull Knife tried to persuade the officers to let him return to Montana. Although treated with kindness and given lodging, Dull Knife's band was not allowed to leave the camp for more than two months. Finally, in January, 1879, the Indians were told that they had to go back to Indian Territory immediately, even though it was the middle of the winter. Dull Knife objected, saying, "That is not a healthful country. . . . We do not wish to go back there and we will not go. You may kill me here, but you cannot make me go back." The government officials at Camp Robinson tried to starve and freeze the Indians into submission. On the night of January 9, the Cheyenne band—which included women and children—made a desperate attempt to flee. They were hunted for 12 days, and most of them lost their lives.

Dull Knife, his wife, his son, and three other Indians were the only ones to escape. After hiding in a cave until the danger was over, they headed north, with only roots, plants, and flowers to eat. When they arrived at the Pine Ridge Agency in the Sioux Reservation in Dakota Territory, they were taken in by sympathizers until it was safe to return to Montana and rejoin Little Wolf at the Tongue River Reservation.

E

EDDY, Mary Baker (1821–1910). Mrs. Eddy founded the Church of Christ, Scientist, which, by the time of her death, had nearly 100,000 members. A frail child subject to fits of hysteria, she was raised as a Congregationalist in New Hampshire. Although her early schooling was irregular, she soon developed a gift for expression that impressed her elders. Widowed in 1844 after less than a year's marriage to Major George Washington Glover, she supported herself by writing magazine articles and substitute teaching. She married again in 1853, this time to a dentist, Dr. Daniel Patterson, from whom she was separated in 1866. The couple divorced seven years later. It was in 1866 that Mrs. Eddy, who was chronically ill, discovered the spiritual system she termed Christian Science. On February 1 of that year, she fell on some ice and suffered internal injuries that left her in critical condition. Three days later, she asked for her Bible and, after reading certain passages, was healed. In recalling this incident, she explained, "My immediate recovery from the effects of an injury caused by an accident, an injury that neither medicine nor surgery could reach, was the falling apple that led to the discovery

how to be well myself and how to make others well." After a period of study, Mrs. Eddy wrote down her religious beliefs in *Science and Health with Key to the Scriptures,* first published in 1875. In this book she described the healing power of mind over matter. "We must understand that the cause and cure of all disease rest with the mind," she wrote. "Disease is caused by mind alone." In 1877, she married one of her religious followers, Asa Gilbert Eddy (1832?–1882), and two years later she organized the First Church of Christ, Scientist (also called The Mother Church) in Boston. She began publishing the *Christian Science Journal* in 1883. The Christian Science Publishing Society, established in 1898, still publishes the *Journal* and other church publications, including a newspaper, the *Christian Science Monitor.*

F

FETTERMAN, William Judd (1833?–1866). An arrogant young army officer, Fetterman was lured into an ambush by the Sioux chief **Red Cloud** (*see*) on December 21, 1866, near Fort Philip Kearny in present-day Nebraska. The entire Fetterman detachment of 80 men was wiped out in one of the most disastrous incidents of the Indian wars. The son of an army officer, Fetterman fought for the Union during the Civil War and was twice breveted for gallantry. In autumn, 1866, he was promoted to captain and transferred to Fort Kearny to serve under Colonel **Henry B. Carrington** (*see*). Fetterman understood neither frontier conditions nor the Indians. He boasted that he could ride through the entire Sioux territory with only 80 men. On December 21, while soldiers from the fort were gathering wood seven miles away, an alarm was sounded that an Indian war party was nearby. Carrington chose Captain J. W. Powell to head a patrol of 80 troops to protect the wood gatherers. Fetterman, who was Powell's senior in service, demanded that he be given command instead. Carrington agreed, but ordered Fetterman to patrol no farther than Lodge Trail Ridge. Ignoring the colonel's orders, Fetterman followed Red Cloud beyond the ridge and into a trap. His entire detachment was massacred in the ambush.

G

GATLING, Richard Jordan (1818–1903). Gatling revolutionized warfare with his invention of the Gatling gun—a multiple-barreled, rapid-fire weapon that foreshadowed the machine gun. The son of a North Carolina plantation owner, Gatling developed his mechanical skill as a youth by helping his father improve agricultural machinery. In later years, he invented several farm implements, including a rice-sowing machine, a wheat drill, and a steam-driven plow. In 1845, after an illness during which he could get no medical attention, Gatling resolved to become a doctor. This he did, receiving his degree in 1850 from the Medical College of Ohio in Cincinnati. However, he immediately returned to mechanical engineering and business in St. Louis and never practiced medicine. Gatling believed that the invention of more terrible machines of slaughter would lead men to abandon warfare. Patented in 1862, his Gatling gun incorporated six to 10 barrels arranged around a central shaft and was operated by a hand crank. Loading and firing—up to 400 rounds

A Gatling gun

a minute—were automatic. The Union Army was reluctant to accept the gun, and it played no important part in the Civil War. The army finally adopted an improved version in 1866. The gun was occasionally used against the Indians and was an important factor in the Spanish-American War. The underworld slang term for a gun—"gat"—derives from Gatling's invention.

GATLING GUN. *See* **Gatling, Richard J.**

GERONIMO (1829–1909). One of the most famous figures of the Indian wars, this Chiricahua Apache chief repeatedly escaped from captivity to renew determined warfare against the white man (*see p. 788*). Born in southern Arizona, he was called Goyathlay —One Who Yawns—by the Indians. He was given the name Geronimo (Jerome) by the Mexicans. As a youth, he fought in war parties led by the Apache chief **Cochise** (*see*). Geronimo's hatred of the white man dated from the slaying of his wife, children, and mother by Mexican soldiers in 1858. Most of the Apaches were forced onto reservations by the early 1870s, but when they were made to relocate at San Carlos, New Mexico, in 1876, Geronimo

escaped into Mexico and commenced hostilities again. Soon captured, he was confined to the reservation until 1881, when he once more took to the warpath. Two years later, he surrendered to General **George Crook** (*see*) and was returned to the reservation. In May, 1885, with a band of renegade braves, Geronimo began a furious rampage that terrorized northern Mexico and the Southwest. For more than a year, federal troops pursued him in vain. Geronimo was finally brought to bay in September, 1886, by General **Nelson A. Miles** (*see*). He was imprisoned at Fort Pickens, Florida, but was eventually allowed to settle at Fort Sill in the Indian Territory (Oklahoma). There he became a prosperous farmer and cattleman and joined the Dutch Reformed Church in 1903. That same year he appeared at the St. Louis World's Fair, and he took part in the inaugural ceremonies of President Theodore Roosevelt (1858–1919) in 1905. The next year, he dictated *Geronimo's Story of His Life,* a defense of the Apache way of life.

Geronimo

GHOST DANCE CULT. This cult of the Plains Indians was a religion that spread rapidly throughout most of the West in the late 1880s. It was started by a Paiute Indian in Nevada named Wovoka (1858–1932). Following an eclipse of the sun on January 1, 1889, Wovoka—or Jack Wilson as he was known to the whites—announced that an Indian messiah was coming who would restore the tribes to their former days of glory. Herded onto reservations and oppressed by the loss of their land, hungry because of the lack of buffalo, and ill with the white man's diseases, the Indians were attracted by Wovoka's promises. According to him, the messiah was to appear in the spring of 1891, and to hasten his arrival the Indians were to perform a religious ritual, the Ghost Dance. The ceremony was always held on five successive nights, during which men and women joined hands and circled around a tree decorated with prayer cloths, singing chants, shouting, and working themselves into a frenzy. Many of the dancers fell into hypnotic trances or had visions in which they supposedly communicated with the spirit world. During the ceremony, the dancers wore white robes or "ghost-dance shirts," which some Indians believed to be magically bulletproof. One of the Arapaho songs chanted at the Ghost Dance reflected the depressed state of the Indians, *"My Father, have pity on me!/I have nothing to eat,/I am dying of thirst—/Everything is gone!"* Suspicious that the Ghost Dance was a war dance and that it would lead to renewed Indian hostilities, the federal government tried to stop performances of the ceremony. When nearly 300 Sioux, who were especially receptive to the religion and were wearing ghost-dance shirts, were slain in the **Wounded Knee Massacre** (*see*) in 1890, the Sioux then ceased to believe in the religion. Other tribes continued to hold the dance, but when the messiah failed to appear in the spring of 1891 as promised by Wovoka, the religion all but died out.

GREAT DIAMOND FRAUD. This spectacular swindle was organized by two miners, Philip Arnold and John Slack, who scattered rough gems—mostly rejected diamonds, rubies, sapphires, and emeralds, which they had bought in Amsterdam, Holland, for $25,000—over a rocky area near a mountain in northern Utah. In the winter of 1872, they quietly spread the word that they had discovered a fabulous mountain containing many types of precious stones. William C. Ralston (1826–1875), one of San Francisco's most reputable bankers, heard of the discovery and saw the opportunity of making a vast fortune. He set up a mining corporation, which included Horace Greeley (1811–1872), then the Democratic candidate for President of the United States. Former General George B. McClellan (1826–1885), who had defeated General Robert E. Lee (1807–1870) at the Battle of Antietam in 1862 and had been the Democratic nominee for President in 1864, was also associated with the corporation. Ralston had Charles Tiffany (1812–1902), the prominent New York jeweler, examine the gems. Tiffany, who had never seen an uncut gem, said that they were "beyond question precious stones of enormous value." He estimated the value of the stones already picked up at $1,500,000. To make sure that the mine was sound, Ralston hired a noted mine expert, Henry Janin, to investigate it. Janin, already convinced by what Tiffany had said, attested to the enormous number of gems that the mine contained. Arnold and Slack subsequently sold their interests to Ralston for $600,000 and disappeared. In the meantime, a geologist, Clarence King (1842–1901), had become suspicious of the gem mountain. He believed that it was a fraud because he had already explored the area and knew that it contained no gems. In November, 1872, after careful investigations, he located the mountain. As promised, the area was scattered with precious stones, including a half-cut diamond. Realizing immediately that the entire affair was a fraud, King announced his discovery and became famous overnight. Slack was never found, but Arnold was discovered in Kentucky, which refused to extradite him. He repaid Ralston $150,000 and was later shot by a business competitor. Ralston, who returned all the investors' money, committed suicide when his Bank of California failed three years later.

H

HARLAN, John Marshall (1833–1911). An Associate Justice (1877–1911) of the Supreme Court for nearly 34 years, Harlan was known as the Great Dissenter because he disagreed with 316 of the 703 decisions in which he participated. Born in Kentucky, Harlan became a lawyer in 1853 and during the Civil War served as a colonel in the Union Army, until he resigned his command in 1863. He then served as attorney general (1863–1867) of Kentucky and ran unsuccessfully for the governorship of his state in 1871 and 1875. As the leader of the Kentucky delegation to the Republican National Convention of 1876, Harlan supported the nomination of Rutherford B. Hayes (1822–1893). The victorious Hayes rewarded Harlan by appointing him an Associate Justice in 1877. Harlan's dissenting votes were, for the most part, based on his firm belief in civil liberties and civil rights, as well as his deep respect for the Constitution. One of the first instances in which he disagreed with a Supreme Court decision was in the so-called Civil Rights Cases of 1883. In a series of five rulings, the Court declared that the Fourteenth Amendment, which among other things, established black citizenship, did not empower Congress to protect blacks from the social discrimination of individuals. Harlan, however, believed that such protection was intended by the framers of the Constitution. Harlan also registered a dissenting vote in *Plessy vs. Ferguson* in 1896. In this case, the majority ruled that blacks and whites should have separate but equal facilities. Harlan believed that such "Jim Crow" laws insured segregation and deprived blacks of full equality. A year earlier, he had disagreed with the majority in *Pollock vs. Farmers' Loan and Trust Company.* The Court held that federal income taxes were unconstitutional. Harlan considered this ruling to be a denial of the federal government's right to levy national taxes. In the so-called Insular Cases of 1901, he objected to the ruling that the Constitution does not necessarily apply to the citizens of new possessions of the United States. Harlan believed that "the Constitution followed the flag," and that all citizens of United States territories should be automatically protected by the Constitution. In other dissenting opinions during his remaining years on the Court, Harlan argued for the limitation of work hours in dangerous or unhealthy occupations. He also believed that the Court had overstepped its authority in 1911 by ruling that the Standard Oil Company of New Jersey had to be dissolved and the American Tobacco Company had to be reorganized. In both cases, the court interpreted the Sherman Antitrust Act of 1890 as a restraint on "every . . . *unreasonable* combination" of trade. Harlan believed that it was not up to the Court to decide what was reasonable or unreasonable. Although Harlan devoted most of his energies to the Supreme Court, he was a member of the 1893 Paris international tribunal that settled the Bering Sea fur-seal controversy between the United States and Britain.

HICKOK, James Butler ("Wild Bill") (1837–1876). Many legends have grown up about Wild Bill Hickok, who was a Union scout during the Civil War and later a frontier marshal. He was born in Illinois and about 1855 moved to Kansas, where he was employed as a constable and a stagecoach driver. Wild Bill got his nickname after being credited with killing an outlaw leader and several members of his gang in 1861. During the war, Hickok was not only a scout but also served as a spy, sneaking behind enemy lines disguised as a Confederate officer. In 1865, he killed Dave Tutt, a fellow Union scout who had turned traitor. After the war, Hickok was appointed deputy marshal at Fort Riley, Kansas, and sometimes scouted for General **George A. Custer** (*see*). He became marshal of Hays City in 1869 and of Abilene two years later. Hickok's gun is often credited with bringing law and order to these frontier towns. Some accounts contend that Hickok left Abilene after mistakenly killing his own deputy. At any rate, in 1872 he toured the East with a Wild West show. Hickok was reportedly arrested several times for vagrancy before he arrived in 1873 in Deadwood, Dakota Territory, with **Calamity Jane** (*see*), whom many thought he had married. While playing poker in Deadwood, Hickok was shot and killed for no apparent reason by a man named Jack McCall. Hickok was holding pairs of aces and eights, and that combination has since been known as the deadman's hand.

Wild Bill Hickok

HILL, James J. (1838–1916). A railroad builder and financier, Hill was known as the Empire Builder for his role in developing the Northwest (*see pp. 802–808*). Born in Ontario, Canada, Hill went to St. Paul, Minnesota, in 1856, where he got a job as a clerk with a Mississippi steamboat line. Nine years later, he went into business for himself as a freight forwarder. In 1872, he consolidated his services with those of **Norman Kittson** (*see*), operating a steamboat service between St. Paul and Winnipeg, Manitoba. Six years later, Hill persuaded three friends—Kittson, George Stephen (1829–1921), and Donald Smith (1820–1914)—to pool their resources to purchase the bankrupt St. Paul & Pacific Railroad. They reorganized it as the St. Paul, Minneapolis & Manitoba Railway Company and extended its tracks to the Canadian border. In the 1880s, the Dakotas and Montana were crossed, and in 1890 the operations were consolidated into the Great Northern Railway, which reached Seattle three years later. Hill had developed a railroad system that stretched from Lake Superior to Puget Sound, one of the greatest achievements in railroad history. By 1901, Hill and John Pierpont Morgan (1837–1913) had gained control of the Northern Pacific. They then purchased the Chicago, Burlington & Quincy Railroad after a bitter financial battle with Edward H. Harriman (1848–1909), head of the Union Pacific, and his backer, **Jacob Schiff** (*see*). In 1905, Hill, with Morgan, organized another railroad, the Spokane, Portland & Seattle line. He retired from railroading in 1912.

HOMESTEAD ACT. This law provided settlers with millions of square miles of free public lands in the West. Legislation of this type had been advocated for years by the Free Soil Party, but Southerners had opposed it, believing that large areas would then be settled by nonslaveholders. In 1860, the Republican Party adopted a free-soil position, and the secession of the South provided the perfect opportunity for passage of the law. The act, which was signed by President Abraham Lincoln (1809–1865) on May 20, 1862, provided up to 160 acres of free land to any man over 21 who established five years' residence and who had not served in the Confederate Army. However, land speculation after the Civil War by railroad companies and wealthy private investors prevented homesteaders from acquiring more than one-sixth of the available land.

J

JACKSON, Helen Hunt (1830–1885). A noted American poet and writer, Mrs. Jackson championed the cause of the American Indian at a time when public sentiment backed widespread efforts to suppress them. Born Helen Maria Fiske in Amherst, Massachusetts, Mrs. Jackson wrote her earliest works either anonymously or under the pen name of Saxe Holm. After the death of her first husband, Edward Bissell Hunt (1822–1863), she began to write poems, which were published in *Verses by H. H.* (1870) and *Sonnets and Lyrics* (1886). She first gained recognition with *Bits of Travel* (1872). In 1875, she married a wealthy Colorado Springs banker, William Sharpless Jackson, and became concerned about the welfare of the Indians in the Colorado area. She sent to every member of Congress at her own expense her tract "A Century of Dishonor" (1881), which dealt with the government's maltreatment of the Indians. As a result, Mrs. Jackson was appointed in 1882 to be a special government commissioner to report on the conditions among the Mission Indians of California. This study inspired her novel, *Ramona* (1884), which is a romantic portrayal of the plight of the Indians. Mrs. Jackson's earlier novel, *Mercy Philbrick's Choice* (1876), is a fictional account of the life of her friend, poet Emily Dickinson (1830–1886).

JEANNETTE DISASTER. The ill-fated steamer *Jeannette* sailed out of San Francisco Harbor on July 8, 1879, to explore the Arctic. The expedition was sponsored by James Gordon Bennett, Jr. (1841–1918), the publisher of the New York *Herald* and son of its founder, James Gordon Bennett (1795–1872). The ship became trapped less than two months later on September 5 in an ice pack 25 miles east of Herald Island in the Arctic Ocean and drifted for nearly two years in its grip. Eventually crushed by the ice, the *Jeannette* sank on June 13, 1881, north of Russian Siberia. Her captain, George Washington De Long (1844–1881), and his 33-man crew trekked over the frozen sea for the next two months, hoping to reach Siberia. When they arrived at open water, the men set out in three boats for the delta of the Lena River. A gale separated the boats on September 12, and one was never seen again. A second craft, commanded by the chief engineer, George Wallace Melville (1841–1912), reached one of the eastern outlets of the Lena River. There the sailors were rescued by inhabitants and made their way to safety through Siberia. The third boat, commanded by De Long, landed farther north in the delta in uninhabited country. De Long and the 14 men with him died, one after the other, of exposure and starvation. In the spring of 1882, Melville headed an expedition that discovered the bodies of De Long's party. He also recovered the captain's journal, which was published in 1883 under the title *The Voyage of the Jeannette.*

JEHOVAH'S WITNESSES. *See* **Russell, Charles T.**

JOHNSTOWN FLOOD. The most destructive flood in the nation's history occurred on May 31, 1889, when a dam burst near Johnstown, Pennsylvania. More than 2,200 people died, 967 others were listed as missing, and property valued at $17,000,000 was destroyed. Johnstown is situated in a valley where the Stony Creek and Little Conemaugh Rivers meet in southwestern Pennsylvania. In the late 1840s, as part of the Pennsylvania canal system, the then largest earth dam in the nation was built, forming a huge artificial lake, Lake Conemaugh. In 1879, wealthy Pittsburghers purchased the lake for use by members of the South Fork Fishing and Hunting Club. Leaks in the dam were patched with straw, stumps, and clay. Floods were not rare in the valley. Serious spring floods had occurred in 1885, 1887, and 1888, but the dam had never given way. An investigation, instigated by the owner of the city's largest steelworks in 1880, found that the dam needed a thorough overhaul, but the club members refused to repair it. Most people did not consider the lake waters a threat to the valley. However, it rained for 11 days during May, 1889, and when the rains came again on May 30, the pressure of the water started to undermine the dam's walls. At 3:10 the next afternoon, the dam broke. In 35 minutes, 20,000,000 tons of water, rushing at an average speed of 40 miles an hour, emptied into the valley, where 30,000 people lived. Debris, including tons of railroad equipment, was picked up and carried forward by the rampaging waters. The next day, when the flood waters began to recede, the valley was strewn with mud, rubble, and corpses. The survivors lacked shelter, medicine, and food. Relief funds in excess of $3,000,000, food, and household supplies poured in from around the world. **Clara Barton** (*see*) came with members of her newly organized American Red Cross and stayed for five months, bringing relief to thousands. Damage claims were filed against the club owners, but a series of juries all ruled that the flood had been a "visitation of Providence." Eventually Johnstown was rebuilt, but for years it was famous as Flood City. Sections of the dam, which was never rebuilt, are now part of a national memorial park.

JOSEPH (1840?–1904). A gentle and peace-loving Indian, this great Nez Perce chief is credited with conducting one of the most brilliant military operations in history. In 1863, the federal government repudiated an earlier treaty and opened for settlement the Wallowa Valley in Oregon, the home of the Nez Perce. By the time Joseph became chief in 1871, the valley was filling with settlers and clashes were increasing. In 1877, Chief Joseph agreed to move his tribe to a reservation in present-day Idaho. During the relocation, however, several of his warriors murdered 18 settlers. American troops were called out, and Chief Joseph found himself committed to the war that he had tried to avoid. After a few battles in which he consistently outfought and outmaneuvered General Oliver O. Howard (1830–1909), Chief Joseph collected about 650 of his tribe—fewer than 200 of them warriors—and started on a remarkable running fight toward Canada. He eluded Howard's forces and defeated General John Gibbon (1827–1896) in a fierce battle at Big Hole River, in what is now Montana, on August 9. He fought his way across southwestern Montana,

Joseph

twice crossed through the Rockies, and forded the Missouri River. In the Bear Paw Mountains, only 30 miles from the Canadian border and safety, Chief Joseph was overtaken by General **Nelson A. Miles** (*see*). Unable to escape without abandoning his wounded and the women and children of his party, Chief Joseph constructed a network of trenches and withstood a five-day siege. On October 5, he walked toward the American lines and delivered his famous surrender message (*see pp. 798–799*). He had fought his campaign for four months over a trail 1,300 miles long. After his defeat, Chief Joseph was sent to a reservation in Indian Territory (Oklahoma) and later to northern Washington. A year before his death in 1904, he visited President Theodore Roosevelt (1858–1919) and General Miles. An officer who had been present at his capture later wrote, "I think that, in his long career, Joseph cannot accuse the Government of the United States of one single act of justice."

JUDSON, Edward Z. C. *See* **Buntline, Ned.**

SMITHSONIAN INSTITUTION: BUREAU OF AMERICAN ETHNOLOGY

K

KING, Richard (1825–1885). A New York-born steamboat captain, King founded the famous King Ranch in southern Texas in the early 1850s. After serving as a pilot on a government steamer on the Rio Grande during the war with Mexico, King settled in Texas, where in 1848 he purchased a small steamboat and became a trader on that river. Two years later, he was a partner and organizer of Kenedy & Company, which built and operated a fleet of steamboats on the Rio Grande until 1872. In 1852, King bought 75,000 acres of land southwest of Corpus Christi, Texas, between the Nueces River and the Rio Grande. Two years later, he established a ranch there, the first in the area. By 1855, the King Ranch covered more than 500,000 acres. During the Civil War, King amassed a fortune as a blockade runner, ferrying cotton from the Rio Grande to Tampico and Veracruz in Mexico, where he exchanged it for supplies for the Confederate Army. Between 1876 and 1880, he built the Corpus Christi and Rio Grande Railroad, which ran between Corpus Christi and Laredo, Texas. At one point, King had 100,000 head of cattle, 20,000 sheep, and 10,000 horses. Before he died, he began to replace his longhorn cattle with superior breeds that he imported. His grandson, Robert J. Kleberg, Jr. (1896–1975), developed a hybrid breed—the Santa Gertrudis—which flourishes in tropical climates. The King Ranch, the largest in the United States, spreads over some 825,000 acres. Gas and oil were first discovered there in 1939; overall royalties from King Ranch energy operations were once estimated to be more than $100,000,000 annually.

KINTPUASH. *See* **Captain Jack.**

KITTSON, Norman Wolfred (1814–1888). Kittson was a successful fur trader who helped to finance the railroad that opened the Red River Valley in present-day Minnesota and North Dakota to settlement. He was born in Canada and went to work at the age of 16 for the American Fur Company. In 1843, **Henry H. Sibley** (*see*) made him a partner in the company. In 1854, Kittson moved to St. Paul and four years later was elected mayor. Kittson became the director of river traffic on the Red River of the North for the Hudson's Bay Company in 1860. Twelve years later, he joined **James J. Hill** (*see*) to form a highly profitable steamboat service on the same river. Together with Donald Smith (1820–1914) and George Stephen (1829–1921), Kittson and Hill bought the bankrupt St. Paul & Pacific Railroad in 1878. Kittson put nearly all of his life savings into the railroad, which was renamed the St. Paul, Minneapolis & Manitoba Railway and ran from St. Paul to the Canadian border. Shortly after the railroad's reorganization, ill health forced Kittson to retire.

L

LITTLE BIG HORN, Battle of the. *See* **Custer's Last Stand.**

LITTLE CROW (1803?–1863). Chief of the Santee Sioux, Little Crow led the most bloody Indian uprising in the history of the frontier (*see pp. 778–779*). Little Crow was the fifth Santee chief in succession to bear the Indian name that means "the sacred pigeon hawk that comes walking." Although not an exceptional warrior, he was a skillful orator and easily persuaded the Sioux to follow him. He adopted white man's clothes and became a Christian. In 1851, the Santee sold part of their land in the Minnesota Territory to the federal government. When an annual payment failed to arrive in 1862, the Sioux, beginning on August 17, went on a six-week rampage known in history as the Minnesota Massacre. About 7,000 Sioux attacked white settlements over a 200-mile area, killing an estimated 700 civilians and 100 soldiers. The uprising was finally put down by troops under Colonel **Henry H. Sibley** (*see*). Of the more than 2,000 Sioux captured, 309 were condemned to die. However, President Abraham Lincoln (1809–1865) commuted the sentences of all but 38 Indians, who were then hanged. Little Crow, who had escaped capture, was shot and killed the following summer when he was discovered picking berries on a farm near the town of Hutchinson, Minnesota.

LITTLE WOLF (dates unknown). A warrior leader of the Northern Cheyennes, Little Wolf fought a series of bloody battles in the late 1870s trying to regain tribal lands in what is now Montana. As chief of a military society known as the Bow String, Little Wolf had led skillful attacks on the Comanches and Pawnees in the 1830s and gained a strong following among his own people. In 1877, along with a large band of Northern Cheyennes under Chief **Dull Knife** (*see*), Little Wolf was persuaded to live among the Southern Cheyennes in Indian Territory (Oklahoma) near Fort Reno. About 18 months later, after suffering illness and starvation, a band of almost 300 Cheyennes organized by Little Wolf and Dull Knife determined to leave to return to their former lands in the Montana Territory. Disobeying government orders, they escaped across the

Plains, fighting off attacks at least four times. After crossing the Union Pacific Railroad line in west-central Nebraska, Little Wolf and 112 Cheyennes separated from Dull Knife to winter nearby. Here they were met by cavalry forces under Lieutenant W. P. Clark, a friend for whom Little Wolf had scouted two years earlier. Clark promised to do all he could to secure the right of the Indians to remain. Because of the fate suffered by Dull Knife's party, public sentiment favored letting Little Wolf and his followers settle in the area. The Tongue River Reservation was established shortly

Little Wolf

afterward for all Northern Cheyenne Indians.

M

McCOY, Joseph G. (1837–1915). In 1867, McCoy bought Abilene, Kansas, and established it as a major shipping point for cattle from Texas. As a prosperous cattleman in Illinois, McCoy recognized that there was a fortune awaiting anyone who could connect the huge supply of cattle in the Southwest with the large markets in the North and East. Accordingly, McCoy journeyed to Abilene, a small town in which the major industry was catching the prairie dogs that destroyed the crops on nearby farms. He bought the town for $2,400 and built a three-story hotel and stockyards. The Kansas Pacific Railroad, somewhat dubious about the project, agreed to give him one-eighth of the profits on each car of cattle shipped. McCoy advertised his stockyards and personally persuaded many Texas cattlemen to drive their stock to Abilene. In his first year of business in 1867, 35,000 cattle were shipped east from Abilene. Soon, the trail from Texas to Abilene, known as the **Chisholm Trail** (*see*), became heavily traveled, and after his second year the railroad owed McCoy $200,000. It reneged on the contract, and he was forced to sue to collect. McCoy later wrote a book, *Historic Sketches of the Cattle Trade of the West and Southwest* (1874). He died in Kansas City on October 19.

MACKENZIE, Ranald Slidell (1840–1889). A highly respected officer in the Civil War, Mackenzie was one of the army's most effective commanders in the postwar struggle to subdue the Indians. An expert in the tactical deployment of troops, he was known to the Indians as Bad Hand because of an injury he had sustained during the war. A native of New York City, Mackenzie graduated at the head of his West Point class in 1862. Immediately assigned to active duty in the Union Army, he fought with valor at Fredericksburg, Chancellorsville, Gettysburg, and in many other important campaigns in the Eastern theater of operations. He was wounded three times in all and was cited for bravery on seven occasions during the war. By the end of it, he commanded a division of cavalry. General Ulysses S. Grant (1822–1885) regarded Mackenzie as "the most promising young officer in the army." After the war, Mackenzie, then a colonel, was assigned to the frontier to pacify hostile Indians. After successful campaigns in Texas and the Indian Territory (Oklahoma), he was sent to fight the Sioux and the Cheyennes in Nebraska and the Wyoming Territory. In the mid-1870s, he helped subdue bands led by **Red Cloud, Crazy Horse,** and **Dull Knife** (*see all*). Mackenzie then commanded operations against the Utes in Colorado and present-day Utah (1879–1881). He retired as a brigadier general in 1884 because of failing health and died in Staten Island, New York.

MANGAS COLORADAS (?–1863). One of the most feared and hated of the Apache chiefs, Mangas Coloradas attacked white settlements in the New Mexico Territory until he was lured to his death. Although he pledged friendship to the Americans in 1846, Mangas Coloradas turned against them when he was bound and whipped sometime in the early 1850s by a group of gold miners who were annoyed by his hanging around their camp. In revenge, he raised a large band of Apaches and mercilessly attacked white communities throughout the territory. In 1863, Mangas Coloradas entered a United States military camp to hold a peace parley. He was arrested, and the commanding officer told his sentries, "Men, that old murderer has got away from every single soldier command and left a trail of blood 500 miles along the stage line. . . . I want him dead!" Later in the evening, one of the guards heated a bayonet and thrust it into Mangas Coloradas' leg. The chief leaped to his feet and was shot. The official report said that he died "while trying to escape."

MENNONITES. The Mennonites who first settled throughout North America in the 18th and 19th centuries were Protestants who traced their religious origins back to the Reformation in Europe. The sect was established in Switzerland in 1525 by Conrad Grebel (1489–1526) and later in Holland during the early 1530s by Menno Simons (1496–1561), the Dutch reformer from whom its name is derived. Mennonites believe in the separation of church and state, baptism for believers only, the right not to bear arms, and the practice of nonresistance. Members of the sect came to America in three principal migrations. A first group of about 5,000 south Germans and Swiss settled between 1683 and 1756 in eastern Pennsylvania and later became known as Pennsylvania Dutch. A second wave, 3,000 strong, left Switzerland and southern Germany to settle in western Pennsylvania, Ohio, Indiana, Illinois, and Iowa between 1815 and 1860. From 1870 to the turn of the century, nearly 20,000 Mennonites migrated from Russia and settled in Manitoba, Canada, and the Dakotas, Minnesota, Nebraska, and Kansas. In the Plains states, they planted a red-kernel wheat they had brought from Russia. The bare prairies were soon transformed into fields of waving grain. Many railroad companies vied to have the industrious Mennonites purchase the large tracts of land adjoining their tracks. There are about 90,000 Mennonites living throughout the United States today. The most conservative members are the Amish, who live principally in Pennsylvania.

MILES, Nelson Appleton (1839–1925). Miles spent nearly half of his 42 years in the army fighting Indians west of the Mississippi. He eventually rose to the position of commander in chief of the army, despite the fact that he had no formal military training. Miles was 22 years old when he joined the Union Army in 1861 after organizing a company of volunteers from his native Massachusetts. Although commissioned a captain, he was considered too young for command duties. However, he soon distinguished himself in battle and was rapidly promoted. He was wounded four times and later received the Medal of Honor for the bravery he displayed at the Battle of Chancellorsville. By 1865, Miles, then 26 and a major general of volunteers, commanded more than 26,000 men as head of the Second Army Corps. After the war, he served briefly as the custodian of Confederate President Jefferson Davis (1808–1889), at Fort Monroe, Virginia. He was reduced in rank to colonel when he transferred to the regular peacetime army in 1866, and three years later he was appointed to command the 5th Infantry in the Indian wars. Miles directed the defeat of the Kiowas, the Comanches, and the Cheyennes. He also forced the Indian leaders **Crazy Horse, Sitting Bull,** and **Joseph** (*see all*) to capitulate in the late 1870s. In 1886, having replaced General **George Crook** (*see*) in the Apache campaign in the Southwest, Miles, by then a brigadier general, tracked down and captured **Geronimo** (*see*). He then suppressed the Sioux uprising in the Dakotas brought on by the **Ghost Dance Cult** (*see*) in the early 1890s. Miles was promoted to major general in 1890 and commanded the troops that put down rioting in Chicago during the Pullman Strike four years later. In 1895, he became commander in chief of the army. Miles was in charge of training and supplying

Today's Mennonites still dress simply and maintain the traditions of their religion.

troops during the Spanish-American War, and he himself led the occupation of Puerto Rico in 1898. He retired in 1903 as a lieutenant general. Miles published two autobiographical works, *Personal Recollections* (1896) and *Serving the Republic* (1911).

MOLLY MAGUIRES. The Molly Maguires was a secret society of Irish-American miners that dominated the coal regions of Pennsylvania from about 1865 to 1877. Its members terrorized other miners, mine superintendents and bosses, and the police. The society was named after a similar goup formed in Ireland in 1843 to intimidate landlords, process-servers, and other officials who harassed the poor. The American version was established in the 1850s, mainly to better the oppressive working and living conditions of coal miners. It gained strength during the Civil War, when it came under the control of criminal elements. After the war, its members resorted to intimidation, arson, and murder, and by 1875 they controlled the miners of Pennsylvania firmly enough to cause a general coal strike in the state. About two years earlier, because of the failure of repeated attempts to suppress the Molly Maguires, Franklin B. Gowan, (1836–1889), the president of the Philadelphia and Reading Coal and Iron Company, asked the noted private detective **Allan Pinkerton** (*see*) to investigate the society. Pinkerton's agent, James McParlan (1844–1919), subsequently gathered enough evidence to bring about 80 members to trial. Among them were two of the society's "bodymasters," or ringleaders—Jack Kehoe (?–1879), who was known as King of the Mollies, and Jimmy Kerrigan, who later testified for the prosecution. A series of sensational

murder trials was held between 1875 and 1877, and 20 members, including Kehoe, were hanged. As a result, the Molly Maguires was completely shattered.

MUIR, John (1838–1914). A botanist and geologist, Muir was one of the first leaders of the conservation movement in America. He emigrated with his father from Scotland in 1849 and settled on a Wisconsin farm. He attended the University of Wisconsin in the early 1860s, but insisted on taking only certain courses, such as chemistry and geology. He left the school in 1863 without receiving a degree. An early interest in botany then prompted him to tour Wisconsin, Illinois, Iowa, and Indiana on foot. He walked even farther in 1867, trekking from Indiana to the Gulf of Mexico. The following year, he arrived in Yosemite Valley, California, and made it his home camp for the next six years. During that time, Muir explored the Northwest, Nevada, and present-day Utah, studying forests and glaciers. He discovered 65

NATIONAL PARK SERVICE

John Muir

residual glaciers in the High Sierras. Alaska then attracted him, and he made his first trip there in 1879. He discovered a number of Alaskan glaciers, one of which was named after him, and explored some upper branches of the Yukon and Mackenzie Rivers. Muir was one of the few survivors of the **Jeannette disaster** (*see*), an expedition to the Arctic in 1879–1881. Throughout his journeys, he recorded his observations and wrote for newspapers and journals. Muir suggested methods to curtail the destruction of forests and vigorously recommended the formation of national parks. In 1889, he helped organize a campaign to establish Yosemite National Park and in 1903 went on a camping trip there with President Theodore Roosevelt (1858–1919). Roosevelt later set aside 148,000,000 acres of public lands for forest reserves. Muir's books include *The Mountains of California* (1894), *Our National Parks* (1901), and *The Yosemite* (1912). The Muir Woods National Monument, a forest of redwoods north of San Francisco, was established by Roosevelt in 1908, six years before Muir's death.

MULLAN, John (1830–1909). An army lieutenant, Mullan supervised the building of a road from Fort Benton in present-day Montana to Walla Walla in what is now the state of Washington. The road, completed in 1863 and known as Mullan Wagon Road, opened that section of the nation to miners and settlers. Mullan graduated from West Point in 1852 and spent the next three years helping to survey a railroad route from St. Paul, Minnesota, to the Pacific coast. While on this assignment, he discovered Mullan Pass in Montana. As chief of construction (1858–1863) on the military road that later bore his name,

Mullan had to fight several battles with Indians. After completion of the road, Mullan resigned from the army to become a rancher and start a mail service between California and Idaho. He later practiced law in San Francisco and Washington, D.C.

O

OKLAHOMA LAND RUSH. On April 22, 1889, about 100,000 settlers—in wagons, on horses, and even on foot—rushed into present-day Oklahoma and claimed 1,920,-000 acres of land. The United States government had purchased parts of the Indian Territory from the Five Civilized Tribes and opened them to settlement under provisions of the **Homestead Act** (*see*) of 1862. The Indian Territory was the last major land area in the continental United States to be opened for settlement. More than half of the Indian Territory belonged to the Cherokees, Choctaws, Creeks, Chickasaws, and Seminoles, who had been forced to move there from the Southeast in the 1820s and 1830s. However, three cattle trails passed through the area, and white men—such as the "Boomers" of the 1880s, who, were removed by the army, and later the "Sooners"—had tried to settle on Indian lands. Thousands of prospective settlers and speculators—attracted to the huge land offerings—lined up along the territory's borders with Kansas and Texas. With the firing of guns into the air at noon on April 22, the rush was on. Each settler, according to the Homestead Act, was allowed to claim 160 acres. The following year, the area was organized into the Oklahoma Territory. Another 100,000 settlers entered during a second land rush in 1893. However, so many had entered illegally before the first rush that

Oklahoma was nicknamed the Sooner State when it was admitted to the Union in 1907.

P

PALMER, William Jackson (1836–1909). Palmer was a railroad builder who began his career as a surveyor's assistant and worked up to be president of a railway. Born in Delaware, Palmer went to work at the age of 17 for the Hempfield Railroad in Pennsylvania. He served as private secretary to the president of the Pennsylvania Railroad, J. Edgar Thomson (1852–1874) from 1858 until the outbreak of the Civil War, when he organized the 15th Pennsylvania Cavalry. Palmer took part in a number of major battles and was promoted to brigadier general in 1864. He was cited for his conspicuous services on several occasions and was awarded the Medal of Honor. After the war, Palmer became treasurer of the eastern division of the Union Pacific Railroad. He directed construction of its line from Sheridan to Denver in present-day Colorado. When it was finished in 1870, he resigned to become president of the new Denver & Rio Grande Railroad.

He left the presidency 13 years later but retained control of the Rio Grande Western, the western section of the line. In the 1880s, Palmer also helped to finance the Mexican National Railway and served as president of that line from 1881 until 1888. In addition, he was instrumental in founding Colorado Springs in 1871. Palmer also helped to establish Colorado College there three years later. He retired in 1901.

PANIC OF 1857. The Panic of 1857 occurred after a decade of speculation in land, railroad construction, and manufacturing that followed the Mexican War and the discovery of gold in California. During that period, the number of inadequately regulated state banks grew rapidly, and these banks were quick to extend credit to wheat farmers seeking new lands in the Middle West. The panic was touched off in August, 1857, by the failure of the Ohio Life Insurance Company, which led to the closing of banks that had heavily invested in it. The only area of the nation untouched by the depression that followed was the cotton belt of the South. Cotton prices remained high. The depression throughout the rest of America

Palmer's Denver & Rio Grande R. R. wound its way through narrow canyons.

Wall Street brokers besiege paper boys for news about the Panic of 1857.

was characterized by unemployment and deflation. The cost of living between 1851 and 1860 rose 12%, while wages rose only 4%. Bread lines formed in Eastern cities, and discontent spread through the Western farm lands. It was against this background of stability in the South and depression in the rest of the nation, and the increasing hostility over the issue of slavery, that the newly formed Republican Party grew. Eastern manufacturers were especially disgruntled by the low tariffs that Southerners had been able to push through Congress. Farmers in the Middle West, stymied by Southern opposition to opening new lands for settlement, also supported the new party, which, in 1860, elected its first President, Abraham Lincoln (1809–1865).

PARKER, Isaac Charles (1838–1896). As a frontier judge, Parker sentenced so many men to death that he was called the Hanging Judge. Born in Ohio, Parker first practiced law in the frontier town of St. Joseph, Missouri. During the Civil War, as a politician in St. Joseph, he worked to keep Missouri in the Union. He was elected to the first of two terms in the House of Representatives in 1870. At the request of anti-Southern Radical Republicans and Parker himself, President Ulysses S. Grant (1822–1885) in 1875 appointed him federal judge of the western district of Arkansas, with jurisdiction over the bordering Indian Territory (Oklahoma). The territory was infamous as a refuge for outlaws, and normal judicial processes had nearly ceased to exist. After establishing his headquarters at Fort Smith, Arkansas, one of Parker's first acts was to appoint 200 deputy marshals. Eight days later, on May 10, 1875, the first of 18 men charged with murder was brought to trial. Six were hanged. A crowd of more than 5,000 people, including newspaper reporters from the East, gathered to witness their execution, and Parker's reputation was established. In the 21 years that he was a judge, 73 more men were

hanged in the district. A certain degree of law and order was established, but, in later years, public sentiment across the nation turned against Parker. Higher courts reversed many of his later sentences. Parker, who was accused of ignoring constitutional safeguards in order to secure convictions, contended that his methods were necessary to bring order to the frontier.

PERALTA LAND FRAUD. Nearly 17,000 square miles of land in present-day central Arizona and western New Mexico were claimed in 1883 under a fictitious Spanish land grant by a swindler named James Addison Reavis (1841–1918?). Reavis was aware that United States courts recognized Spanish land-grant claims under certain conditions, and so he set out to fabricate such a claim. In 1876, he acquired a fraudulent deed to a grant of land. The deed purported to assign land in central Arizona to Miguel Peralta of San Diego, heir of the original grantee, Don Miguel de Peralta, who had allegedly been given the land by the king of Spain in 1757. Reavis stretched

The self-styled Baron of Arizona, Reavis claimed that the Peralta Grant covered an area almost equal in size to the states of New Hampshire and New Jersey combined.

the property from its original claim of about the size of Delaware to an area equal to the states of New Jersey and New Hampshire combined. After years of research and compiling false papers, he filed his claim in 1883 with the surveyor general of the Arizona Territory. The United States government was stunned. Reavis was claiming land that ran from the junction of the Gila and Salt Rivers to west of Silver City, New Mexico, and from Four Peaks to Picacho Pass, Arizona. Panicky settlers offered to buy or lease rights from Reavis to remain on their land. The Southern Pacific Railroad paid him $50,000 for the right to run tracks across the property, and mining companies also paid the swindler for rights to work their land. The Silver King Mine alone gave him $25,000 in order to continue its operations. To make his claim ironclad, Reavis reared a half-breed orphan named Sophia Treadway (1862–?) and presented her to society as Doña Sofia, the sole remaining heir of Don Miguel. He then married the girl. Between 1883 and 1895, Reavis—who was dubbed the Baron of Arizona—lived in a style befitting his title. He was feted by New York society leaders, and his wife was presented to the royal court in Spain. Meanwhile, the State Department sent two special agents to Spain and a third to Mexico to verify the documents on which Reavis based his claim. They found that all the documents were forged. Don Miguel, his descendants, and his estate had never existed. The Peralta claim was officially proved faudulent in the Court of Special Land Claims in Santa Fe in 1895. Reavis was tried for conspiracy and convicted the following year. He served nearly three years in prison before his release in 1898. Reavis, who was divorced by Sophia, died in obscurity about 20 years later.

PESHTIGO FIRE. On October 8, 1871—the same evening that the **Chicago fire** (*see*) occurred—a forest burst into flame around Peshtigo, Wisconsin, killing nearly 1,200 people, almost five times as many as were lost in Chicago. A sma!!, backwoods lumber town on the Peshtigo River, six miles from Green Bay, Peshtigo had one telegraph wire connecting it with the outside world. With construction under way on a railroad line connecting Peshtigo to the sawmill industries of Menominee, Michigan, and Marinette, Wisconsin, the future of the town looked promising. However, the slash, or wood debris, that the railroad gangs set on fire helped to destroy it. The summer of 1871 had been an especially dry one, with only one rain shower falling throughout July, August, and September. On October 8, the sun seemed to disappear at midday and an odd, yellow glow lighted the town. By dinner time, ashes were blowing through screenless kitchen windows and getting into food. About nine o'clock that evening, the deep, moaning sound of approaching flames could be heard in Peshtigo. Slabs of fire began to fall from the sky, and then a sudden wind swept through the town. The fire spread and destroyed a sawmill, a factory, homes, churches, and the ione telegraph wire. By 10 o'clock, Peshtigo was completely leveled. The only survivors were those who had managed to reach the river. A second fire destroyed the nearby villages of Williamsonville, New Franken, and Robinsonville. Together, the two fires burned 1,280,000 acres of woodland and farms and caused nearly 1,200 deaths. On October 9, a rain fell, 26 hours too late to avert the disaster.

PICKETT, Bill (?–1932). A black cowboy, Pickett, was the most famous bulldogger in the West. He was one of the thousands of

Only those who reached the Peshtigo River survived the disastrous fire of 1871.

blacks who went to work for ranchers after the Civil War. A native of Texas, Pickett signed on as a cowhand at the sprawling 101 Ranch in Oklahoma in the late 1890s. The hands of the 101 were the most skillful around, consistently victorious at amateur rodeos. In 1905, the Miller brothers, who owned the 100,000-acre ranch, decided to organize their own rodeo. Pickett, a spectacular bulldogger, quickly became the show's top drawing card. Not only could Bill "take down" a steer in record time, but he could also do it without using his hands. Leaping from his saddle onto a racing animal, he would wrestle the steer's head upward, grab its upper lip between his teeth, and bring the startled beast thudding to earth by rolling off the side. The Miller troupe was soon booked far and wide. On opening night at Madison Square Garden in New York City, Pickett's steer bolted from the chute, hurdled a six-foot fence, and charged through the crowd. Pickett and his horse followed. So did Will Rogers (1879–1935), the entertainer and humorist, who was also with the troupe. Amid the screaming spectators, Pickett bulldogged the unruly animal, and Rogers hog-tied it. Appearing in Mexico City in 1908, Pickett accepted a challenge to ride a fighting bull. With several thousand screaming, bottle-throwing Mexicans demanding blood—Bill's—Pickett survived six punishing minutes aboard the indignant toro. After the rodeo closed in 1914, Bill worked on the Miller ranch. In 1932, when he was over 70 years old, Bill was stomped to death by a wild horse.

PIKES PEAK HOAX. The Pikes Peak Hoax—or Pikes Peak Humbug, as it was also known—was an exaggerated discovery of gold in 1858 at Cherry Creek in present-day Colorado, 75 miles from Pikes Peak. The discovery of gold eight years earlier at Ralston Creek, near the present site of Denver, had prompted several prospecting parties to organize in 1858 for a more thorough search of the Rockies. They did find gold at Cherry Creek, but so little of it that 57 of the original 70 prospectors turned around and went home. However, the news of their discovery was exaggerated by newspapers, and inflated tales of the reputed goldfields filled the pages of the nation's journals during the winter of 1858–1859. Guidebooks for inexperienced Plains travelers were also published, advising the best routes to the gold fields. This publicity, coupled with the widespread unemployment that followed the **Panic of 1857** (*see*), resulted in a stream of eager gold seekers in the spring of 1859. They crossed the prairies on foot, on horseback, and in wagons often painted with the slogan "Pikes Peak or Bust." The majority returned east—without gold—within a few months, those who retained their sense of humor writing "Busted by Gosh" on their wagons for the trip home. In May, 1859, some gold was found in the Gregory Lode nearby, and a second gold rush began. Again, most prospectors found only disappointment and by the end of the summer were on their way back east.

PINKERTON, Allan (1819–1884). This Scottish-born sleuth founded a famous detective agency and during the Civil War was influential in organizing a counter-espionage department that later became the Secret Service. After immigrating to America in 1842, Pinkerton settled in Illinois, where in 1846 he was appointed deputy sheriff of Kane County. Four years later, he became the first detective of the Chicago police force and founded a private detective agency, which, in 1852, became Pinkerton's National Detective Agency. It soon gained national prominence for solving a series of robberies that were plaguing train and express companies. In 1861, while engaged in railroad detective work, Pinkerton claimed to have discovered a plot to assassinate President-elect Abraham Lincoln (1809–1865) as he passed through Baltimore on his way to his first inauguration. He organized Lincoln's secret night ride through that city on February 22–23 and foiled the plot. From the beginning to the end of the Civil War, Pinkerton organized a spy system behind Confederate lines, which he headed under the assumed name of Major E. J. Allen. After the war, he resumed his position as president of his agency and opened branches in New York and Philadelphia. Between 1874 and 1876, his agency, through the work of one of its detectives, James McParlan (1844–1919), broke up the **Molly Maguires** (*see*), a secret terrorist organization of Pennsylvania coal miners. After 1877, Pinkerton, who believed that unions were damaging to workers, was active in strikebreaking and gained a reputation for the harsh methods he and his agents used during a series of railroad strikes. He completed the last of 18 books he wrote about his detective work just before his death in 1884. The agency—which was continued by his sons, Robert A. Pinkerton (1848–1907) and William A. Pinkerton (1846–1923)—gained further notoriety when its agents, known as Pinks, broke up the famous 1892 Homestead Strike against the Carnegie Steel Company. The agency, which changed its name to Pinkerton's, Inc., in 1965, is still one of America's leading private detective services.

California prospectors wash gold they have extracted from a placer mine.

PLACER MINES. These mines are above ground or near the surface, and the minerals mined from them require no digging. They are found loosely packed in sand or gravel. Because the minerals are heavier than the sand or gravel, they can be removed by panning, sluicing over an inclined trough, washing by hand, or, more recently, by washing with a machine. The most common minerals found in placer mines are gold, platinum, tin, chromium, and precious stones. Placer mining was the method used by the first prospectors in California, and later by prospectors during the **Pikes Peak Hoax** (*see*) in 1858–1859 and during the gold rush in the Klondike and Alaska, 1897–1898.

PLEDGE OF ALLEGIANCE. The Pledge of Allegiance to the Flag was first published in a children's magazine, *Youth's Companion,* on September 8, 1892. It was printed in leaflets and distributed to more than 12,000,000 schoolchildren, who took the pledge during the celebration of the 400th anniversary of Columbus' discovery of the New World on October 12, 1492. In the original pledge, reference was to "my flag." This was changed to read "the flag of the United States of America" in 1923. After a long dispute, the United States Flag Association, a private patriotic organization, decided in 1939 that the pledge had been written by Francis Bellamy, a staff member of *Youth's Companion,* rather than by the editor, James Upham. The pledge was officially adopted by Congress in 1942 during World War II. Twelve years later, President Dwight D. Eisenhower (1890–1969) approved the adoption of the phrase "under God" into the pledge. The pledge, with the addition, reads:

I pledge allegiance to the flag of the United States of America and to the Republic for which it stands, one Nation under God, indivisible, with liberty and justice for all.

PONY EXPRESS. The Pony Express, which operated from April, 1860, to October, 1861, was an overland relay mail-carrying service between St. Joseph, Missouri, and Sacramento, California. Despite its brief existence, it remains one of the most colorful episodes in the history of the West because of the bravery and devotion of its riders, who risked their lives in treacherous weather conditions and in hostile Indian country in order to deliver the mail. After gold had been discovered in California in 1848, Westerners put pressure on Congress to authorize plans for a swift mail route to the West Coast. In 1858, the Southern Overland Mail Company, operated by John Butterfield (1801–1869), began a postal stagecoach service over a southern route between St. Louis and San Francisco that took from 22 to 25 days. However, many people believed that a central route would be quicker. Early in 1860, William H. Russell (1812–1872) of the well-known Missouri freighting firm of Russell, Majors and Waddell, organized the Pony Express to demonstrate the practicality of a central route. He hoped to win for his company a profitable mail-carrying contract from the government. When it was inaugurated on April 3, 1860, the Pony Express carried mail weekly to and from California, and the service later became semiweekly. About 75 horses were used in each direction. It generally took 10 days to cover the full distance of nearly 2,000 miles from St. Joseph to Sacramento via Cheyenne, Salt Lake City, and Carson City. The best time the Pony Express ever made was when it carried the First Inaugural Address of President Abraham Lincoln (1809–1865) in seven days and 17 hours. Its riders, who rode at a steady gallop where possible, changed mounts in under two minutes at stations that were set up at 10- or 15-mile intervals along the route. After a run of anywhere between 40 and 125 miles, a rider handed over his saddlebags to another horseman, who then continued on. Although riders were frequently killed or wounded, the Pony Express operated day and night all year round and is reputed to have missed only one trip during its 18 months of operation. The expenses of the service were enormous, and the venture was a disastrous financial failure. When the first telegraph hookup between the Missouri River and California was completed on October 24, 1861, the Pony Express ceased its operations. After the outbreak of the Civil War in 1861, the Southern

Overland Mail operated a daily mail-carrying coach service on the central route established by the Pony Express. The line was purchased the following year by the financier Ben Holladay (1819–1887). In 1866, he sold out to **Wells Fargo** (*see*), which for many years after the completion of the Union Pacific Railroad in 1869 continued the service of the Overland Mail to areas not reached by the railroad.

PRAIRIE SCHOONER. The prairie schooner was a type of covered wagon that received its name because, from a distance, its white canvas, horseshoe-shaped cover resembled the seagoing schooners of the 19th century. It was first used in the Santa Fe trade in the 1820s. Later, the prairie schooner became the traveling home of Mormons, prospectors seeking gold in California, and settlers moving to Oregon. It was still used in freighting operations in the Great Plains as late as the 1880s. The schooner was a descendant of the earlier and heavier Conestoga wagon. It was

A prairie schooner

drawn by teams of oxen or mules. A settler's wife and children usually rode in the interior, receiving light and air through the oval openings at each end of the wagon's covering. When they crossed the Great Plains, pioneers in prairie schooners often traveled in groups, or caravans, known as wagon trains in order to protect themselves from outlaws and hostile Indians. A trip from west of the Missouri River to the Pacific

Northwest would take four to five months.

R

RED CLOUD (1822–1909). Chief of the Oglala Sioux, Red Cloud (*see p. 782*) directed the two-year Indian campaign (1866–1868) that forced the United States to abandon the **Bozeman Trail** (*see*) and the three forts that were built to protect it in the Powder River country of present-day Montana and Wyoming. Red Cloud was born in what is now Nebraska. His father was named Lone Man, and his mother was Walks as She Thinks. As a warrior, Red Cloud was fierce and brave and "as full of action as a tiger." He led both Sioux and Cheyenne braves in raids so effective that the federal government was compelled to negotiate a treaty in 1868. On December 21, 1866, Red Cloud's band wiped out the 80-man detachment of Captain **William J. Fetterman** (*see*) near Fort Philip Kearny, Wyoming. However, on August 2 of the following year, soldiers equipped with new repeating rifles killed or wounded nearly 200 of his warriors in the famous Wagon Box battle (*see p. 793*). After 1868, Red Cloud worked for peace with the white man. Admired for his dignity and character, he opposed "civilization" but later accepted certain Christian doctrines. In 1881, after demanding the ouster of an Indian agent, he was deposed as chief of the Oglalas by the federal government. Red Cloud died at the age of 87 on an Indian reservation in South Dakota.

REMINGTON, Frederic Sackrider (1861–1909). Remington was a New York-born painter, illustrator, writer, and sculptor who is best-known for his portrayals of

life on the Western frontier. After studying at the Yale School of Fine Arts (1878–1880), Remington visited the West and made sketches and gathered material on which he later based his realistic paintings and drawings of cowboys (*see pp. 745, 752–753, and 760–761*), Indians (*see p. 727*), soldiers, frontiersmen (*see frontispiece, Volume 6, and p. 537*), and horses (*see pp. 762–763*). After additional study at the Art Students League of New York, Remington returned to the West, where he began doing illustrations of frontier scenes. During the Spanish-American War, he worked in Cuba as an illustrator (*see p. 997*) and war correspondent for the Hearst newspaper chain. Remington also traveled widely in Europe, Asia, and North Africa and by the turn of the century was one of America's leading magazine illustrators, contributing to such periodicals as *Harper's Weekly, Collier's Weekly,* and *Century.* He also produced a notable series of bronze sculptures. Among the books that Remington wrote and illustrated are *Pony Tracks* (1895), *Crooked Trails* (1898), *Sundown Leflare* (1899), *Stories of Peace and War* (1899), *Men with the Bark On* (1900), *John Ermine of Yellowstone* (1902), and *The Way of an Indian* (1906). His picture portfolios include *Drawings* (1897), *Remington's Frontier Sketches* (1898), and *Done in the Open* (1902). The Remington Art Memorial Museum at Ogdensburg, New York, houses many examples of his work.

RENO, Marcus (1835–1889). At the Battle of the Little Big Horn in 1876, Reno commanded a battalion that was forced to retreat and consequently failed to support troops led by **George A. Custer** (*see*). Although a court of inquiry later absolved Reno, many people

Reno's retreat across the Little Big Horn was depicted on buffalo hide by a Sioux.

continued to blame him for Custer's defeat. A graduate of West Point (1857), he served as a Union officer during the Civil War and was later transferred to the West. On June 25, 1876, Custer gave Reno, then a major, command of three companies and ordered him to cross the Little Big Horn River in present-day Montana. Indians attacked Reno's battalion shortly after it crossed the river. During the battle, a scout standing next to Reno was shot in the head, and Reno was badly unnerved. Outnumbered 10 to 1, he ordered a retreat. Reno's men recrossed the river and took refuge on a bluff. More than half the battalion had been killed, wounded, or left behind. Troops commanded by Captain Frederick Benteen (1834–1898) soon arrived to reinforce Reno. For all practical purposes, Benteen assumed command. Both men expected help from Custer momentarily. The Indians kept Reno and Benteen pinned down until the following afternoon. Not until they were relieved on June 27 did they discover what had happened at **Custer's Last Stand** (*see*). Reno was later accused of cowardice for ordering the retreat, but a court of inquiry cleared him of the charge in 1879. Following

an incident at a frontier post, Reno was court-martialed and dishonorably discharged in 1880 for engaging in a drunken brawl, although five of the seven members of the court had urged clemency in his case. In 1967, a descendant appealed to the army to clear Reno's name and restore him to full rank. On May 31 of that year, his army record was corrected to read that he was honorably discharged as a major.

REYNOLDS, Joseph Jones (1822–1899). From 1872 to 1876, during the bloody fighting between soldiers and Sioux on the northern Plains, Reynolds successively commanded Fort McPherson, Nebraska; Fort D. A. Russell, Wyoming; and the district of South Platte. Reynolds graduated from West Point in 1843. He returned there three years later as a member of the teaching staff, remaining until 1855. After two years at Fort Washita, in Indian Territory (Oklahoma), Reynolds left the army to teach mechanics and engineering at Washington University in St. Louis. In 1860, he opened a grocery in Lafayette, Indiana. When the Civil War began, Reynolds helped organize the Indiana Vol-

unteers. In 1862, he was appointed to a divisional command in the Army of the Cumberland, with the rank of major general. Reynolds fought in the Battles of Chickamauga and Chattanooga in 1863, and the following year, as a corps commander, he was in charge of the defense of New Orleans. After the war, he held commands in Texas before being transferred to the Nebraska Territory in 1872. The defeat of Reynolds' cavalry at the hands of **Crazy Horse** (*see*) in March, 1876, took place three months before the death of **George A. Custer** (*see*) and his men at the Little Big Horn River (*see* **Custer's Last Stand**). Reynolds was suspended from command afterward and retired from the army the following year. He settled in Washington, D.C.

RICHARDSON, Henry Hobson (1838–1886). Richardson was an architect whose designs dominated the emerging cities of Chicago, Cincinnati, Cleveland, and St. Louis in the late 19th century. He

Henry Hobson Richardson

graduated from Harvard in 1859 and went to Paris, where he studied at the Ecole des Beaux-Arts. Quite successful, Richardson was urged to remain in France and become a citizen, but he returned to America in 1866. His reputation spread quickly. Critics consider Trinity Church in Boston, completed in 1877, his best work. The style he developed became known as Richardson Romanesque. In later years, he turned from church architecture to the design of private homes and public buildings such as libraries, railway stations, and city halls. Among other structures, Richardson designed the Marshall Field Building in Chicago. Although he was acclaimed as the foremost American architect of his day, after his death his style was poorly imitated and condemned as too ornate, expensive, and unsuited to American tastes. However, more recent critics have labeled Richardson the nation's first functional architect and a creative genius.

RUSSELL, Charles Taze (1852–1916). Russell founded the religious sect known as Jehovah's Witnesses. A native of Pittsburgh, Russell, who supported himself by selling shirts, broke away from the Congregational Church in 1872 after becoming convinced that there was no Biblical authority for the concept of eternal damnation. Organizing a group of followers known as Russellites, he preached that the Second Coming of Christ and the millennium—when Christ would rule on earth—were imminent. Although he had no formal religious training, Russell adopted the title of pastor in 1878. His teachings were spread in the *Watch Tower,* a newspaper he founded that same year. In the 25 years between 1881 and 1906, Russell compiled his most important writings into a six-volume series entitled *Studies of the Scriptures.* In later years, his public reputation was marred by personal scandals associated with his divorce in 1909 and the sale, two years later, of a "miracle" wheat to his followers. However, the religious sect he founded continued to grow. He opened a meetinghouse called a tabernacle in Brooklyn in 1909 and one in London in 1911. Congregations of Russellites were established throughout the United States, Canada, and Europe. In 1931, the sect formally adopted the name Jehovah's Witnesses. There are approximately 700,000 "ministers" (members) throughout the United States.

S

SAND CREEK MASSACRE. In early November, 1864, about 700 Indians, most of them Southern Cheyennes led by Chief **Black Kettle** (*see*), established a village on Sand Creek, in what is now eastern Colorado. The government had asked friendly Indian tribes to make camp near army forts so that they could be distinguished from warring Indians in the area. Black Kettle desired peace, and he had been assured by officers at nearby Fort Lyon that his people could live on Sand Creek without army interference. However, at dawn on November 29, Colonel **J. M. Chivington** (*see*) launched a surprise attack on the encampment with about 750 volunteer cavalrymen. Chivington, a former clergyman who hoped to further his political ambitions by defeating the Indians, ignored a flag of truce and ordered that all inhabitants of the village be slain. At least 160 Indians, two-thirds of them women and children, were killed. Black Kettle's wife was shot nine times. The soldiers then took dozens of scalps, which they exhibited several weeks later at a Denver theater during an intermission. Most of the Southern Cheyennes who escaped fled north and renewed war with white settlers, although a few, including Black Kettle, continued to seek peace. News of the Sand Creek Massacre—widely regarded then by whites as well as Indians as the white man's most shameful act of savagery during the Indian wars —sent many Plains tribes on the warpath.

SATANK (?–1871). Satank was an important chief of the Kiowas in the Southwest. Together with **Satanta** (*see*), he bitterly resisted

Satank

efforts to confine his tribe to a reservation. Satank's Indian name was Setangya, or Sitting Bear. He was the leader of a fierce Kiowa military fraternity called the Kaitsenko. The bearded and mustachioed chief was much feared among his people because he was surly and vengeful. In addition, the Kiowas believed Satank possessed superhuman powers. After his son was killed during a raid in 1870, the chief always carried the child's bones, bundled in a blanket, into battle. In May, 1871, Satank and Satanta were arrested after they attacked a wagon train near Fort Richardson, Texas. While being transported to Jacksboro, Texas, Satank began singing the death song of the Kaitsenko. Knowing he would be killed but determined not to be imprisoned, Satank wrenched off his handcuffs and attacked and wounded his guard with a concealed knife. He was shot to death by another soldier.

SATANTA (?–1878). A leader of the Kiowas in the Southwest, Chief Satanta—which means White Bear—was famed both as a warrior and as an orator. Unlike his evil-tempered fellow chief, **Satank** (*see*), the eloquent Satanta was loved and respected by the Kiowas. Satanta, who liked to announce dinner in his village by blowing a French horn, was at first friendly to the white man. In April, 1864, he cooperated with the government in having his tribe vaccinated against smallpox. However, hostilities soon broke out because of a misunderstanding when the Kiowas approached an army fort in peace but were shot at. Although Satanta declared that he would not remain within the Kiowas' assigned area in Indian Territory (Oklahoma)—"I love to roam over the prairies," he said—he nevertheless signed a treaty with the federal government accepting the restriction in 1867. In 1871, Satanta, Satank, and two other chiefs were charged with attacking a wagon train in Texas. Satank was killed in an attempt to escape. Satanta, who had proudly admitted the deed, was taken to Jacksboro, Texas, where he was condemned to be hanged. President Ulysses S. Grant (1822–

1885) intervened, and the sentence was commuted to life imprisonment. Under pressure from the Department of the Interior, the Texas governor paroled Satanta in October, 1873, after he had been imprisoned for two years. The Kiowa chief, who was well over 60 years old, soon began leading his tribe again in attacks on invading buffalo hunters. In 1874, Satanta was apprehended a second time. He was taken to the Texas state prison at Huntsville. Four years later, he jumped to his death from a window.

SCHIFF, Jacob Henry (1847–1920). One of America's foremost bankers and philanthropists, Schiff was involved in the financing of some of the major railroads in the East, notably the Pennsylvania Railroad and the Baltimore & Ohio Railroad. However, the most spectacular episode in his financing career took place in 1901 when, in partnership with Edward H. Harriman (1848–1909) and backed by John D. Rockefeller (1839–1937), he tried to gain control of the Northern Pacific Railroad from **James J. Hill** (*see*) and John Pierpont Morgan (1837–1913). The struggle between the two rival groups was so intense that the price of Northern Pacific stock soared to $1,000 a share and provoked a brief financial panic in May of that year. Neither side won, and a friendly settlement was reached later that year with the formation of the Northern Securities Company, which was a holding company owned by the two groups. It controlled the Great Northern, the Northern Pacific, and the Chicago, Burlington & Quincy Railroads. Because Harriman controlled the Union Pacific and Southern Pacific Railroads as well, the company had a virtual monopoly on the transportation facilities in the West. Be-

cause the Northern Securities Company represented an alliance of the greatest financial figures in the nation, President Theodore Roosevelt (1858–1919), believing that it would stifle competition, challenged its legality under the Sherman Antitrust Act in 1902. His position was upheld by the Supreme Court two years later in the first major antitrust victory in American history. The company was dissolved. Schiff had begun his career as a broker after he immigrated to the United States from Germany in 1865. By the time he was 38, he was head of the New York brokerage firm of Kuhn, Loeb & Company. Besides financing railroad projects, he had large interests in several major manufacturing companies, notably Westinghouse Electric and Western Union. In addition, Schiff was involved with insurance companies, including the Equitable Life Assurance Society, of which he was director. He was generous with the great wealth he amassed, and his charitable activities were varied and numerous. Schiff was particularly concerned with Jewish philanthropies. He endowed the Jewish Theological Seminary in New York, the Semitic Museum at Harvard University, and in 1906 helped to found the American Jewish Committee, a charitable organization. He was also active in the Red Cross and founded or promoted many libraries, schools, settlement houses, and hospitals, including Montefiore Hospital in New York City.

SEWARD'S FOLLY. *See* **Alaska, Purchase of.**

SIBLEY, Henry Hastings (1811–1891). After the Minnesota Massacre in 1862—during which the Santee Sioux under **Little Crow** (*see*) went on a six-week rampage—Sibley, who had no prior military experience, was appointed to command the state militia organized to fight the Sioux Indians. He had begun his career as a clerk for the American Fur Company and had then become a partner in one of its branches operating in the Wisconsin and Dakota Territories. Sibley came to know the Sioux well and enjoyed a great deal of prestige among them. In 1849, he promoted the organization of the Minnesota Territory and served as a territorial delegate (1849–1853) in Congress. When Minnesota became a state, Sibley was elected the first governor (1858–1860). He was commissioned a colonel in 1862 and, after leading successful expeditions against the Sioux, was commissioned a brigadier general in 1863. Sibley and his men captured more than 2,000 Indians, tried by court-martial more than 400 of them, and executed 38 (*see p. 779*). From 1865 to 1866, Sibley helped to negotiate treaties with several of the Sioux tribes. Except for one term in the state legislature in 1871, he spent his remaining years occupied with private business interests and also served as president of the board of regents of Minnesota University.

SITTING BULL (1834–1890). A highly revered Hunkpapa Sioux chief and medicine man, Sitting Bull has become a symbol of the Plains Indians who struggled to preserve their traditional way of life in the late 19th century. Until the summer of 1874, the Sioux had roamed freely over the Powder River region in present-day Montana, South Dakota, and Wyoming. That year, Colonel **George A. Custer** (*see*) found gold in the Black Hills in South Dakota, an area promised to the Sioux forever under a treaty signed at Fort Laramie, Wyoming, in 1868. Prospectors rushed to the area and

pressured the government to open it up for settlement. The government ordered all the Indians to report to agencies on their reservations by January 31, 1876. Sitting Bull and others were apparently

Sitting Bull

unaware of the order, and when troops under Colonel **Joseph J. Reynolds** (*see*) attacked a friendly Indian camp in March, 1876, the tribes went on the warpath. Because of his magical powers—he could reputedly heal the sick and

see into the future—Sitting Bull gained great influence among his people. In a ritual ordeal, he had his arms and chest cut all over to induce bleeding and a trance. During the trance, he saw white soldiers falling into the Indians' camp. The chief's vision came true at the Little Big Horn River on June 25, 1876, when Custer and nearly 250 cavalrymen were wiped out by a combined force of Sioux and Cheyenne warriors under Sitting Bull's leadership (*see* **Custer's Last Stand**). The Sioux chief then became one of the government's prime targets, and troops were sent after him by General **Nelson A. Miles** (*see*), who tried to persuade the chief to go to a reservation. "God Almighty make me an Indian and not an agency Indian," Sitting Bull responded. He fled into Canada in 1877 with a small band. However, because there were no buffalo to hunt, he led his band back south in July, 1881, surrendering at Fort Buford in present-day North Dakota. Two years later, Sitting Bull moved to the nearby Standing Rock Reservation, and in 1885 he toured with Buffalo Bill Cody's Wild West Show. The fear that the new **Ghost Dance Cult** (*see*)—which preached the coming of an Indian messiah who would restore the old way of life—would lead to renewed hostilities prompted the government to arrest Sitting Bull in 1890. The army was afraid that he might lead the Indians into war again. Early on the morning of December 15, government-paid Sioux Indian police employed by the **Bureau of Indian Affairs** (*see*) marched into his cabin on Standing Rock Reservation and ordered him to dress. The protesting chief was led outside, where he was surrounded by followers. One of them shot the Indian police lieutenant, who then turned and shot Sitting Bull in the stomach. At the same time, another policeman shot the chief in the back of the head. A number of other Sioux were also killed in the incident, including Sitting Bull's son. The death of Sitting Bull broke the spirit of the Sioux, and most of them moved back to their reservations.

STANTON, Elizabeth Cady. *See* **Anthony, Susan B.**

STARR, Belle (1848–1889). Described as "The Petticoat Terror" and a "bandit queen," Myra Belle Shirley, better known as Belle Starr, gained notoriety as an alleged horse and cattle thief, a suspected stagecoach robber, a prostitute, and a protector of outlaws. The Missouri-born Belle began her varied career in the late 1860s in a Dallas saloon, dealing poker and faro. After two years at the card tables, she left the saloon to marry an outlaw, Jim Reed, with whom she fled to California to escape arrest. The couple went back to Texas in the early 1870s, and Belle returned to the gambling houses when her husband was killed in 1874. She then had six successive common-law husbands, all of whom were outlaws and five of whom were Indians. In 1889, Belle's body was discovered in the mud at the edge of a road near her ranch near Eufaula in present-day Oklahoma. She had been shot in the back with a double-barreled shotgun. Both her son, Ed Reed, and her neighbor, Edgar Watson, were suspected of the murder, but the case was never solved. Belle's illegitimate daughter, Pearl, also a prostitute, buried her mother with Cherokee rites and had a bell and star carved on her tombstone.

SULTANA DISASTER. One of the worst disasters in steamboat history occurred when the 1,719-ton side-wheeler *Sultana* exploded and burned on the Mississippi River in the early morning hours of April 27, 1865. About 1,700 persons were killed in the disaster. The *Sultana* had sailed with a crew of 85 from New Orleans on April 21 north to Vicksburg, then a center for repatriated Union prisoners of war. Despite her legal capacity of 376 people, the ship took on more than 2,000 soldiers at Vicksburg, many of them gaunt survivors of Confederate prison camps. She then fought an unusually strong current upriver to Memphis, where repairs were required on one of the ship's boilers. Leaving Memphis late at night on April 26, the *Sultana*'s captain, J. C. Mason, remarked, "I'd give all the interest I have in this steamer if we were safely landed at Cairo!" However, while still only a few miles from Memphis, the

Flung into the icy Mississippi River when the Sultana *exploded in April, 1865, many Union soldiers drowned.*

boilers suddenly exploded near a group of islands called "the Hen and Chickens." The orange-colored flame that shot into the night sky could be seen in Memphis. The *Sultana* was almost blown apart by the explosion. Hundreds of soldiers were thrown into the icy river, where many of them, too weak to swim, drowned as hot coals showered down upon them. Others still on board were burned to death. One survivor reported afterward that he "could see men jumping from all parts of the boat into the water, until it seemed black with men, their heads bobbing up like corks, and then disappearing beneath the turbulent waters, never to appear again." The *Sultana*, her twin smokestacks collapsed and her superstructure caved in, drifted downstream to a small island where the few men remaining on board made her fast. There, the still-smoldering hulk sank. The morning light revealed the Mississippi filled with survivors hanging onto debris and its banks dotted with burned men. Between 500 and 600 victims were rescued, but 200 among them died from burns. In all, between 1,500 and 1,900 lives were lost in the disaster. For days afterward, a Memphis barge was sent out every morning to collect the bodies. Despite the enormity of the catastrophe, the loss of the *Sultana* received little newspaper coverage because America's attention was focused on the closing days of the Civil War.

T

TIMBER CULTURE ACT. The Timber Culture Act, which was passed by Congress on March 3, 1873, allowed any homesteader to increase his landholding by 160 acres if he agreed to plant trees on at least 40 acres of his newly ac-

quired acreage. According to the **Homestead Act** (*see*) of 1862, any settler over 21 years of age was allowed 160 acres of free land. However, homesteaders in the Dakotas, Nebraska, and Kansas soon discovered that 160 acres was not enough land on which to raise livestock and engage in successful farming operations. This was because the region had few trees and little rainfall and was plagued by hot winds that caused dust storms. In the 1870s, many people believed that growing trees would increase the humidity in the air and thereby encourage additional rainfall. Accordingly, Congress passed the Timber Culture Act, which was specifically designed to encourage settlers in the Dakotas, Nebraska, and Kansas to grow trees in the region. Although 10,000,000 acres were given to homesteaders under this law, the grants were widely abused by land speculators. It was also difficult to grow trees in the arid Great Plains, and in 1878 the tree-growing requirement was lowered from 40 to 10 acres. On March 3, 1891, the act was repealed.

TREATY OF WASHINGTON. Signed on May 8, 1871, the Treaty of Washington established an important precedent for the peaceful settlement of disputes between the United States and Great Britain. Two disputes—the rights of American fishermen in Canadian waters, and the ownership of San Juan Island, situated between the state of Washington and British Columbia —had preceded the Civil War and were revived shortly after the war's end. However, these were overshadowed by a third dispute. The American government demanded that Britain repay the damages done during the war by the *Alabama* and other Confederate cruisers built on British soil (*see* **Alabama claims**). Britain re-

fused to even discuss the claims after there was talk in the United States that only the territorial cession of Canada could fully repay the direct and indirect damages. Hamilton Fish (1808–1893), who became Secretary of State in 1869, indicated a more conciliatory attitude in private talks with a Canadian, Sir John Rose. With Rose acting as intermediary, Britain's foreign minister, Lord Granville (1815–1891), agreed to the establishment of a Joint High Commission to meet in Washington, D.C., with an open agenda. The first meeting was held on February 27, 1871, at the State Department. Although the negotiations were held in secrecy, Fish was careful to keep influential Senators informed of their progress. The final agreement, reached 10 weeks later, was ratified in the Senate by a vote of 50 to 12 on May 24, 1871. The resolution of the *Alabama* claims was of paramount interest in both nations. An international tribunal, with representatives from the United States, Britain, Italy, Brazil, and Switzerland, was designated to arbitrate the claims. The treaty's preamble contained a British confession of guilt for allowing the cruisers to be built, as well as an apology. To guide the work of the arbiters, three rules of international law governing neutrality were agreed upon by Britain and the United States. In addition, Canadian and American fishermen were granted reciprocal fishing rights. Because this benefited the United States, an international commission was established to determine what the United States would have to pay for the fishing rights. Emperor William I (1797–1888) of Germany was named arbiter of the boundary dispute. On October 21, 1872, he announced his decision to grant San Juan Island to the United States.

TURNER, Frederick Jackson
(1861–1932). One of America's
most influential historians, Turner
revolutionized the study of American
history with his paper on
"The Significance of the Frontier
in American History." It was first
delivered as a speech on July 12,
1893, at a meeting of the American
Historical Association at the
Chicago World's Fair. Before
Turner's paper, the study of
American history centered on the
actions of individuals and four
great themes—the desire for religious
freedom, the revolt against
British tyranny, the admiration
for democracy in the writings of
European philosophers such as
John Locke (1632–1704), and sectionalism.
Relying heavily on
economic and geographic data,
Turner accepted the role of sectionalism,
but could not find in
the other theories the forces that
had shaped America. How, Turner
asked, could people, often from
autocratic or feudal backgrounds,
create a democracy with free social
and political institutions? He
found the answer in the frontier
and in the cheap land beyond it.
For three centuries, he said, land-
hungry immigrants had come to
America. Because the power of
the government was weak on the
frontier, these people had been
forced, by trial and error, to
create a way of life totally unlike
Europe, in which self-reliance was
the chief virtue. Turner had
studied at the University of Wisconsin,
from which he received a
Bachelor of Arts degree in 1884
and a Master of Arts degree four
years later. He subsequently taught
history there (1889–1910) and at
the same time studied at Johns
Hopkins University for his doctoral
degree, which he was awarded
in 1890. Turner next taught history
at Harvard University (1910–
1924), and afterward he was a research
associate at the Henry E.

Huntington Library in San Marion,
California. His address of
1893 was reprinted, along with
other essays, in *The Frontier in
American History* (1920). He also
wrote *The Rise of the New West*
(1906), which dealt with the frontier
and sectionalism. Sectionalism
was further discussed in *The Significance
of Sections in American
History* (1932) and *The United
States, 1830–1850: The Nation
and its Sections* (1935). Turner's
use of economic and geographic
data is now accepted by all leading
scholars, although his frontier
thesis has been criticized by some
20th-century historians.

W

A Wells Fargo stagecoach

WELLS FARGO. Wells, Fargo &
Company—popularly known simply
as Wells Fargo—was the
major express service and bank in
the Far West during the second
half of the 19th century. It was
founded in 1852 by Henry Wells
(1805–1878) and George Fargo
(1818–1881), who were, respectively,
the president and the secretary
of the American Express
Company, which had been established
in 1850 as an express service
in the East. Soon after the
California gold rush of 1849, the
two men realized that they could
reap considerable profits by transporting
gold from California to
the East. Unable to persuade the
board of American Express that
this would be a lucrative under-

taking, they decided to establish
a separate enterprise on their own
and opened an office for banking
and express business in San Francisco
in July, 1852. Four years
later, it was California's leading
bank and express company. At
first, American Express and Wells
Fargo acted as allies, with American
Express handling operations
in the East, and Wells Fargo those
in the West. Eventually, however,
the two companies became competitors.
For many years, Wells
Fargo's main operations were
shipping and banking transactions
for miners. Its postal service
carried mail to miners in places
not reached by the government
mails. The stagecoach was one of
the most common means of transportation
employed by Wells
Fargo, and in 1866 the company
bought up most of the major
stagecoach lines operating between
the Missouri River and California.
However, after 1869, when
the first transcontinental railroad
was completed, Wells Fargo ceased
most of its stagecoach operations,
except in places where tracks did
not exist, and began buying rail
express rights. By 1888, the firm
had acquired enough rail express
services to become the first transcontinental
railroad express agency.
Because of their great value,
Wells Fargo cargoes were frequently
robbed. One of the most
notorious bandits to prey upon its
stagecoaches was "Black Bart, the
Po8 [a code word for *poet*],"
whose real name was Charley
Boles (1830–?). He never robbed
any other express company, and
he always wore a flour sack over
his head as a disguise and brandished
a double-barreled shotgun
(which was actually unloaded). In
the eight years before he was finally
captured in November, 1883,
he held up 28 stagecoaches. Wells,
Fargo & Company continued its
banking and express operations

until 1905, when the bank became a separate institution that is now the Wells Fargo Bank and American Trust Company. Its express operations were merged with other companies in 1918 to form the American Railway Express Company. The Wells Fargo Armored Service Corporation continues to operate a delivery service.

WOMAN SUFFRAGE. *See* **Anthony, Susan B.**

WOUNDED KNEE MASSACRE.
On December 29, 1890, at Wounded Knee Creek, near Pine Ridge in present-day South Dakota, an entire band of Sioux was slain by the troops of the Seventh Cavalry in the last major incident of the Indian wars. By the 1880s, most of the Sioux Indians in the Dakotas, including their chief, **Sitting Bull** (*see*), were living quietly on res-

ervations. However, in 1889, Indian nationalism was revived by the **Ghost Dance Cult** (*see*). Fearing that the Indians intended to go on the warpath, the army in the fall of 1890 sent 3,000 troops to reservations in the Pine Ridge area in order to keep the peace. Panicked by the appearance of the troops, about 2,000 Sioux moved from their reservations to the Bad Lands, farther east. There they were joined by 1,000 more tribesmen. The army believed that the Indians were planning to fight. Although Sitting Bull had not joined the fleeing Sioux, the army was afraid he would lead them into battle anyway. General **Nelson A. Miles** (*see*) dispatched a detachment to arrest the Sioux chief. Confronted at his camp on December 15, 1890, Sitting Bull refused to be arrested. He was then shot and killed. Shortly after

his death, about 340 more Sioux, led by Chief Big Foot, fled into the Bad Lands, hoping to join the Indians already there. However, they were captured on December 28 by about 200 soldiers of the Seventh Cavalry and taken to a trading post named Wounded Knee. On the next day, when the soldiers tried to disarm Big Foot's followers, a young, apparently insane Sioux fired a single shot into the troops, which now numbered 470. The soldiers returned the fire with their repeating rifles, slaughtering about 300 of the Indians, including 200 women and children. Sixty soldiers died or were wounded, many of them shot by their fellow troopers in the confusion. On New Year's Day, 1891, following a blizzard, the dead Indians were buried in a long pit on the site. Those who were wounded were left to perish in the cold.

Chief Big Foot lies frozen where he was shot to death during the Wounded Knee Massacre of 1890.